Historic Theaters of
YOUNGSTOWN
—— and the ——
MAHONING VALLEY

Historic Theaters of
YOUNGSTOWN
—— and the ——
MAHONING VALLEY

SEAN T. POSEY

THE
History
PRESS

Published by The History Press
Charleston, SC
www.historypress.net

Copyright © 2017 by Sean T. Posey
All rights reserved

First published 2017

ISBN 978-1-5402-2563-4

Library of Congress Control Number: 2017938352

This book is dedicated to the memory of my grandparents,
Rose and Roger Ridder and Irene Posey.

CONTENTS

Contents

ACKNOWLEDGEMENTS

W riting a book of this kind requires the kindness of strangers and a great deal of support from loved ones. I would like to thank my mother, Kathleen, and father, Fred, for their unwavering support. I would also like to thank my uncle, Bryan "Dew" Ridder, for all his kindness and support. Local historian Mark Peyko deserves my gratitude for all the time and attention he has given to my many questions. Videographer Ron Flaviano's tremendous work has been instrumental in helping to publicize this book. I would also like to express my gratitude to the reference librarians at the Youngstown Public Library, especially Sally Freaney. Their tenacity in tracking down obscure historical details helped make this book possible. Thomas Molocea and the Mahoning Valley Historical Society have my unwavering gratitude for providing some rare photographs of Youngstown's historic theaters.

I would also like to thank the following for many of the wonderful photos in this book: Patricia Ringos Beach, Doris and Frank Cavanaugh, Barbara Emch, Ron Flaviano, Girard Historical Society, Vince Guerrieri, Mary Ann (Stabile) Lark, Emanuel Mageros, Mike Parise, Mark Peyko, Struthers Historical Society and Marian Kutlesa, Victory Christian Center and the *Warren Tribune*.

The following individuals kindly took the time to share with me their memories of the many valley theaters: Denny Brayer, Jack Carlton, Doris and Frank Cavanaugh, Bill DeCicco, Frank "Big Daddy" Delio, Mary Ann Flaviano, Ron Flaviano, Sally Freaney, Sharon Williams Garfield, Mark Hackett, George "Viking" Hall, Jaime Hughes, Bryan and Roger Jones,

ACKNOWLEDGEMENTS

Mary Ann (Stabile) Lark, Emanuel Mageros, Candace "Candee Reign" Mauzy, Liz Moore, Mike Petrello, Mark Peyko, William S. Peyko, Fred Posey, Mike Roncone, Thomas Rowe, Richard Scarsella, Bob Vargo and Helga Wengler.

Introduction

FROM THE WARNER BROTHERS
TO BURLESQUE

AN UNLIKELY THEATER TOWN

The village of antebellum Youngstown, Ohio, seemed an unlikely setting for a theater town. Home to fewer than three thousand souls, Youngstown had one small walk-up theater—Arms Hall. The coming of the Civil War brought a new impetus to the area's growing iron industry, linked to outside markets by first the Pennsylvania and Ohio Canal and later the railroads. Eventually, Youngstown became a city and the governmental seat of Mahoning County. With economic and population growth came the first real stage theaters: Excelsior Hall and its successor, the Grand Opera House. Vaudeville and traveling plays provided entertainment for a restive population accustomed to brutally hard labor and the economic insecurity that came with the boom-and-bust iron economy.

Theatrical figure Teddy Joyce once remarked, "Youngstown is a hard town to make laugh, I believe I understand why. People work unusually hard here. They are physically exhausted, and laughing is just a bit more difficult. Especially in times of economic depression, people are more skeptical."[1] Traveling vaudevillians also found Youngstown audiences to be extremely tough crowds, so much so that when they encountered difficult audiences in other cities, performers proclaimed that they were in "another Youngstown, Ohio."[2] The city's extremely heterogeneous population, increasingly composed of scores of foreigner workers, often missed the subtext and humor of American stage performances; many could barely speak English. All of that began to change with the arrival of moving pictures.

The first public exhibition in the early 1890s of Thomas Edison's Kinetoscope, a primitive device that allowed a single person to view a display of simple moving images through a peephole, heralded the bare beginnings of the motion picture craze that would capture the imaginations of Americans and the world in the early twentieth century. By the early 1900s, the dusty streets of Youngstown had been replaced by a rapidly growing urban core surrounded by an ever-growing skyline of buildings and enormous blast furnaces. Immigrants poured into the city seeking jobs in the steel mills, which were visible from nearly every street downtown. Increasingly visible on downtown streets were numerous nickelodeons—spawned by Edison's invention—that provided cheap entertainment.

"The smoking factories wanted young men who could take suffering and keep their woes to themselves," film mogul and onetime Youngstown resident Jack Warner later recalled.[3] Many of those men (and women) relieved their own suffering, if only momentarily, watching the simple films presented in local arcades. Places such as Dreamland, the Star Theater, the Edisonia, the Luna and the Dome Theater drew in the curiosity seekers and the work weary. The economy and the nascent moving picture industry boomed.

The number of nickelodeons nationally doubled between 1907 and 1908 to eight thousand.[4] By 1910, the annual payroll for Youngstown as a whole was larger than Buffalo, Detroit and Toledo.[5] This environment nurtured the entrepreneurial talents of the Warner brothers, who used the knowledge they acquired about the moving picture business in the Mahoning Valley to build one of the most powerful film studios in the world. Rae Samuels, a confidante of the Warners, launched her career from Youngstown to national fame as the "Blue Streak of Vaudeville." The nation's top performers (Al Jolson, Lillian Russell, Maude Adams, Ethel Barrymore and more) graced the stage of the famous Park Theater, which included George M. Cohan as one of its initial investors. In the least likely of settings, industrial Youngstown became a theater town.

As motion pictures began to dominate, early theaters spread to communities throughout the Mahoning Valley. From the A-Mus-U in Struthers to the Palace in Hubbard, neighborhood theaters served walkable communities, becoming as much a part of the landscape as the local cobbler and grocer. In Warren, the second-largest city in the valley, the Warren Opera House, the Hippodrome and eventually the Robins Theater served a growing industrial community.

After vaudeville faded in the early 1930s, the "big four" downtown movie theaters dominated Youngstown: the Palace, which also hosted

Rose and Roger Ridder walk past the Park Theater marquee in downtown Youngstown, circa 1940. *Courtesy of the author.*

music and live acts on its stage; the State Theater; the Paramount; and the Warner Theater. Between 1920 and 1930, only Dayton surpassed Youngstown in population growth among Ohio cities.[6] Every one of the largest production houses (Paramount-Publix, Fox, RKO and Warner Brothers) operated movie houses in the city, giving Youngstown access to as many first-run films as Cleveland or Pittsburgh.[7] The Regent, Cameo and Strand also provided entertainment for those seeking to escape the doldrums of the Depression in the city's darkened theaters.

Vaudeville disappeared, but the art form it spawned, burlesque, thrived in Youngstown during the 1930s and beyond. The always controversial world of burlesque dancing brought lonely sailors and military men into the packed houses of the Princess Theater and the Grand Burlesk during the 1940s, even as the city periodically threatened to shut them down. Vivacious ladies could be seen gracing the stages of the Princess, Park and Grand Theaters, as well as the halls of the Tod Hotel, where so many often stayed. Youngstown gained a reputation as a burlesque town, and with good reason.

All the top dancers, from Toledo's Rose La Rose to Irma the Body (both of whom danced controversial shows that led to the banning of burlesque in Boston), played the steel city. By 1959, Youngstown had become one of the few cities of its size with two downtown burlesque houses—the Strand Theater and the Park Burlesque. After the original Park building fell during urban renewal in 1968, the theater lived on for a time as the "New Park Burlesk" on West Federal Street, memorably known for featuring the famous Sandra "Busty Russell" Churchey.

As the old Park Burlesque building faced the wrecking ball in 1968, the famed Warner Theater closed. In 1970, the State met the same fate. At the end of 1975, the Paramount, the last theater downtown, closed. Two separate developments crippled the downtown movie palaces: suburbanization and the rise of the drive-in theater. The immediate postwar era witnessed the rise of the outdoor auto theaters, as they were often called. Located far from crowded downtowns, drive-ins proved to be the perfect venues for growing families of the baby boom era. The underdeveloped outskirts of Youngstown and Warren saw the opening of no fewer than nine drive-ins in the years after 1940. Today, Ohio remains the state with the second-largest number of outdoor theaters in the country. The Elm Road Triple Drive-In and the Skyway Drive-In keep the Mahoning Valley tradition alive today.

The growing suburbs eventually encroached on cheap, plentiful land that made developing drive-ins so appealing. Plaza theaters drew movie patrons (along with shoppers) away from city business establishments, especially in downtown Warren and Youngstown. The Southern Park Mall and the Eastwood Mall challenged downtown retailers and theaters. Plaza theaters and twin cinemas located in malls had none of the grandeur of the downtown movie palaces—they were much more modest affairs, lacking any of the symbolism and ornamentation of the neoclassical theaters of old. No longer could most people walk to a neighborhood theater conveniently located in a dense, walkable community. The malls replaced the downtown shopping districts, and their cinemas replaced the thousand-seat movie palaces of old.

Youngstown and surrounding communities have changed beyond recognition since the days of the Warner brothers. The Mahoning Valley today, like so many deindustrialized communities in America, is struggling with abandoned properties and shrinking neighborhoods. Most of the old theater buildings have been torn down; those that survive face an uncertain future. The storied legacy of local theater history lives on in those buildings that still stand today. Urban planners and anyone interested in urban revitalization would do well to consider the future of places such as the old Uptown, Foster and the beautiful Robins Theater in downtown Warren.

Part 1

THE BIRTH OF LOCAL THEATER

From the Stage to the Nickelodeon

In about 1855, the first traveling theater troupes journeyed to the village of Youngstown to play Arms Hall, located on the southeast corner of Phelps and Federal Streets. A small space situated on the third floor of the Arms block, the hall hosted comedians, proto-vaudeville acts and minstrel shows. Joseph Jefferson, who became famous for his onstage portrayal of Rip Van Winkle, once played Arms Hall.

Tremendous demand for iron during the Civil War had pushed Youngstown's population to more than eight thousand by 1870. The influx of new residents soon necessitated a much larger space than Arms Hall, so a group of investors purchased the estate of Caleb Wick at the corner of West Federal and Hazel Streets (the future site of the Liberty/Paramount Theater) and built the Excelsior block. The entire third floor of the new building was given over to Excelsior Hall. With footlights, the ability to bring in more complicated sceneries and drop curtains, the Excelsior served as Youngstown's first modern playhouse. It was the most modern theater located between Cleveland and Pittsburgh when it opened.[8]

The Excelsior became known for hosting Thomas "Blind Tom" Wiggins, one of the most widely known American pianists and composers of the nineteenth century. Charles "The Great" Blondin—an acrobat and daredevil who crossed the Niagara Gorge on a tightrope in 1859—attracted one of

Excelsior Hall provided Youngstown with its first proper live theater in the 1860s. *Courtesy of Mahoning Valley Historical Society.*

the largest crowds in Youngstown history when he walked from the Excelsior block across West Federal Street to the Gerstle block on a tightrope. In the late 1860s, the *Youngstown Vindicator* began to print ads for the Excelsior, the very first theater listings to appear in the paper. By the 1870s, however, the burgeoning city was ready for an even larger theater, one becoming to a "kingdom in iron," as Youngstown came to be known by the 1870s.

In 1874, at the southwest corner of Central Square, the Grand Opera House opened to an overawed city. Constructed by local African American architect P. Ross Berry, it could hold two thousand patrons at maximum capacity. The Stambaugh, Tod, Wick and Bonnell families financed the project. The first of its kind in the area, it provided a new outlet for many of the city's well-heeled residents, who had been forced to journey to Cleveland or Pittsburgh to see many shows.

The dome of the building featured an enormous cut-glass chandelier, and a horseshoe-shaped balcony was situated underneath with two boxes on either side of the stage. The stage itself was thirty-five feet deep and seventy-five feet wide. Underneath the boxes by the stage were two elegant eagles carved in wood and several Roman soldiers; each held gaslights used for illumination throughout the theater. Without any kind of stage entrance, sets had to be brought in through the front of the building. Unlike later motion picture theaters, the building lacked a pitched floor, which often resulted in obstructed views, usually from the large, elaborate hats worn by many of the lady patrons. The city eventually attempted to enforce a law regulating the height of hats allowed in local theaters.

The stage's grand drop curtain featured a depiction of Aurora, the Roman goddess of dawn, complete with chariot and cherubs. The subject matter, along with the house's architecture, echoed the classical world. During dark scenes of dramatic tension, the stage manager controlled many of the gaslights to lower the illumination. However, if turned too low, the gaslight would go out, necessitating the halting of the show until they could be relit. Ushers, using long poles, stood above the audience to reach many of the lights.

The Grand Opera House attracted "road shows," which usually played for one night only. *Richard the III*, *The Merchant of Venice* and *Uncle Tom's Cabin* were typical productions staged at the opera house. Repertoire opera companies came from all over. During circus season, when local hotels were packed, players occasionally slept in their dressing rooms. The biggest stars of the day appeared on the house's stage: Edwin Booth, one of the most famous actors of his day and the brother of John Wilkes Booth, as well as "Buffalo Bill" Cody and a young George M. Cohan all played the opera house. Joe Shagrin, area manager who later opened the Foster Theater on the south side, got his start at the Grand Opera House.

Although the opera house attracted the local society crowd, it was also known for raucous behavior. The "Gallery Gods" were rowdy patrons who never failed to show their pleasure or their contempt for a show. As with the efforts to regulate large hats, the city passed an ordinance against peanut eating—which often ended with some Gallery Gods throwing them toward the stage. But this behavior remained part of early theater culture, according to the *Youngstown Vindicator*: "In bygone days the Gallery Gods paid a dime or a quarter for admission, according to the supposed importance of the booking. They never removed their hats, they chewed tobacco, ate peanuts, drank pop and if they didn't like a show they considered it their right to stomp their feet, whistle, hiss or boo. While they reserved such treatment for shows which they referred to as 'cheese,' they were generous in their applause and cheered for shows which they called 'the goods.'"[9]

The nation's top theatrical and vaudeville acts played Youngstown's Grand Opera House during the late nineteenth and early twentieth centuries. *Courtesy of Mahoning Valley Historical Society.*

Moving Picture Theaters

The world of stage entertainment changed irrevocably with the coming of "moving pictures" during the early twentieth century. Crude and simple at first, film gradually became more sophisticated and narrative driven by the end of the second decade of the twentieth century. Eventually, the new medium challenged live theater for the loyalty of local audiences.

In 1894, the first Kinetoscope parlor opened in Manhattan. Author David Robinson described the simple system of viewing moving pictures: "The pictures were on a continuous ribbon of 35mm film threaded on rollers inside of the box. The customer started the machine with a coin (a nickel or a dime) and watched the film through a magnifying lens in an opening on top."[10] In 1896, Koster and Bial's Music Hall in New York publicly premiered the Vitascope, a primitive means of projecting film negatives. The audience, there for a vaudeville show, instead became entranced by the Vitascope's depiction of waves crashing on a beach, which inspired a loud ovation. Nine years after that remarkable demonstration, the first nickelodeon opened in Pittsburgh.

"Nickelodeon" was a generic term used to describe a wide variety of storefront theaters that showed short films. Usually located in busy downtown areas, they exploded in popularity in the years after the opening of the Nickelodeon Theater in Pittsburgh, commonly acknowledged as the first, in 1905. Located some sixty miles away from Pittsburgh, Youngstown also became a hotbed for the early nickelodeons. The exteriors of the storefront theaters varied widely in appearance, from the very crude with simple signage to the more sophisticated theaters with potted plants and simple columns or archways. Phonograph attachments often played songs to attract the attention of pedestrians.

A column from a February 1907 edition of the *Youngstown Vindicator* described the early arcades and five-cent theaters located in the central business district: "At all hours they seem to do a good business, although at night they seem to attract the largest crowds. Some people in Youngstown make a tour of all of the theaters once every week, at least. There are not as many penny arcade shows as there are 5-cent theaters. Another big arcade in Central Square opened its doors to the public only a few days ago."[11]

By late 1907, "Moving Picture Row," as it became known, could be viewed in the area around West Federal and Hazel Streets. Six theaters operated in the area, which took on a carnivalesque atmosphere at night.[12] Storefront theaters also emerged on East Federal Street and on the "Diamond," as

An unknown nickelodeon in downtown Youngstown advertises a film about the kidnapping of young Billy Whitla, a sensational story in Ohio in 1909. *Courtesy of Thomas Molocea.*

Central Square was then called. The city's moving picture houses increased rapidly, and local tastemakers questioned whether Youngstown had gone "amusement mad."

The Lyric Theater, which could seat four hundred, opened on the future site of Home Savings and Loan. The same owners also operated the Alvin Theater, the Lyric's sister house. Other theaters of the time included the Dreamland, Star, Casino, Crescent, Edisonia and Nixon— one of the earliest theaters located on the future site of the State Theater. The Luna, Roma, Luxor and Napoli catered primarily to the growing Italian population in Youngstown. In 1909, Youngstown claimed more theaters than Grand Rapids, Michigan, despite having about thirty-three thousand fewer residents.[13]

Youngstown had indeed gone amusement mad for the new nickelodeons. In 1907, *Motion Picture World* reported a story from Youngstown about an elderly couple attending a local theater. When they were told by management that the show would be delayed for at least two hours due to faulty wiring, the gentleman replied, "If that's the case, I guess me and mother will make ourselves comfortable. We drove six miles this morning, and we are going to see the show before we go home."[14] The story suggests that even the well heeled (few could afford a car in 1907) also attended local moving picture houses, even if they were loath to admit it.

The city's moving picture houses, like elsewhere, varied widely in quality and safety. As the caliber of the theaters improved, advertisements often touted the quality of the ventilation systems in particular buildings—with good reason. Youngstown's nickelodeons were often outright dangerous. The city's board of health considered the air in most to be "as bad as in a sewer."[15] Many nickelodeons were also serious firetraps.

Youngstown's theaters avoided cataclysmic fires like the 1903 Iroquois Theater conflagration in Chicago that claimed the lives of more than six hundred people. But minor fires and explosions did occur. Some houses, such as the Palace Theater in Campbell during the 1930s, would become known for their frequent fires. In 1912, a projectionist at the Lyric Theater received severe burns after an explosion in the projection booth. Accidents of this nature plagued many local theaters for years. According to historian David Robinson, "Fire was only one of the dangers to which [projection] operators were exposed, working often twelve hours a day, practically without relief, in hot, oppressive boxes with dangerous and potentially lethal fumes, carbon and asbestos dust."[16]

Youngstown's first moving picture houses relied heavily on street-level advertising, which included primitive signage and simple theatrical storefronts. *Courtesy of Thomas Molocea.*

Early moving picture shows progressed from very simple one-reel films that were only minutes long to multiple-reel films that might last an hour. Piano players often accompanied these films; later machines such as the Peerless "automatic orchestra" were also used. Peerless machines played in a variety of Youngstown theaters, including the Alhambra on Market Street, the Hillman Theater on Hillman Street and the Mock in Girard. The *Youngstown Vindicator* reported average daily attendance in 1909 at five hundred for the city's smaller moving picture houses and a high of nearly four thousand a day for the larger theaters.[17]

Patrons could expect to see a wide variety of films and subjects, from "fireman films," which depicted scenes of fire departments battling blazes, to some of the most popular narrative films of the time: *A Trip to the Moon*, *The Great Train Robbery* and *The Conquest of the Pole*, among others. The 1903 film *The Life and Passion of Christ* was one of the most popular of the early films, screening in moving picture houses around the country. It played locally at several theaters downtown and at the Erdelac Theater in the Monkey's Nest neighborhood.

Despite the potential for high profits, theater owners paid dauntingly high taxes. In 1910, *Moving Picture World* reported that Youngstown's theater taxes were the highest in the world.[18] The tax amounted to $3 a day at a time when admission usually varied from five to ten cents per person. After much political pressure, the city council voted to adjust licensing rates in 1915. The new rates changed from a flat $50-per-year licensing fee for every theater, including live theaters, to new rates based on size: large theaters paid more than $100, and smaller theaters paid between $25 and $50. This often resulted in theaters with capacity numbers like 299—one short of moving into another tax bracket.

Even with such hurdles, moving picture houses continued to thrive. In late 1911, the city featured several top theaters dedicated to films. The Orpheum Theater, located where the State Theater would later be built, could hold 299, with standing room capable of holding another 200. A block away stood the Star Theater; two storefronts away was the Lyric. The Bijou Theater operated at 4 West Federal Street. Built for $14,000, the theater's lobby consisted of white marble leading to an auditorium capable of seating 196 patrons. Management hid the Bijou's projectionist booth behind a trellis, which unfortunately was filled with asbestos. The Bijou also featured a piano player and a Wurlitzer organ. Daniel Robins, later the head of Robins Enterprises, managed the theater—making it one of the more upscale establishments in Mahoning Valley at the time.

The Bijou Theater was operated at various times by some of the Mahoning Valley's best-known theater managers, including Joe Trunk and Daniel Robins. *Courtesy of Thomas Molocea.*

The Palace Theater (not to be confused with the later Palace on Central Square), located at 11 East Federal Street, represented one of the city's more "respectable" early theaters. Patrons flocked to the Palace, according to theatergoer Carl Straley: "The Palace, another long, narrow, nickel, just east of the square, was generally packed to the doors with patrons....Signs all over the front of the theater informed the general public that Charlie Chaplin, or Snub Pollard, or Ben Turpin, or maybe Fatty Arbuckle was the stellar attraction there."

Billed as "the house beautiful," the Palace featured a fireproof projectionist booth, a finely built lobby and room for 290 patrons—just short of the 299-seat limit on the tax code for midsized entertainment houses. The floor sloped downward to the curtain to prevent obstructed views. Audiences also enjoyed a Wurlitzer orchestration and a three-piece orchestra that provided musical accompaniment. In 1912, the theater featured film taken downtown and throughout the area called *Moving Pictures of Our City*. Being able to see scenes of life in Youngstown on the screen must have been a tremendous novelty, drawing the curious into the theater. Later, films of boxing matches (a very popular attraction at many theaters) packed eager audiences into

The original Palace Theater represented one of Youngstown's finest early moving picture houses. *Courtesy of Thomas Molocea.*

the Palace. The tradition of showing fight films in local theaters continued into the 1960s at places such as the Regent and Paramount Theaters.

Efforts to censor films were more common in Youngstown than in many other places, despite the city's notorious reputation for being "wide open" when it came to vice. The Youngstown Ministerial Association led an investigation into the ten moving picture theaters in the city in 1911, finding that although most of the theaters had poor lighting and ventilation, the pictures shown did not appear to be "highly objectionable."[19] Despite that fact, Youngstown theaters regularly showed films depicting scenes of disaster in the news.

Moving Picture World argued against the screening of such material, but in Youngstown, the mayor himself approved such films.[20] Films on the infamous Triangle Shirtwaist Factory fire, the Collinwood school fire and especially the sinking of the *Titanic* drew large audiences. The *Titanic* disaster fascinated Youngstown. (Local industrialist George Wick perished on the ship.) The Bijou, the Air Dome Theater and others screened footage under titles such as *Blizzard on the Sea* and *The Great Titanic Disaster*. At the Air Dome, advertisements read, "Showing the peril those people were in while on the *Titanic*'s voyage; something you've never experienced." For audiences accustomed to only reading about disasters in newspapers, these films provided a whole new dimension to the news.

As film historian Richard Abel pointed out, the largest theaters in the city at this point were all live theaters: the Grand Opera House, Park Theater and the Princess. Very few theaters operated in the city outside of downtown Youngstown (those that did seldom lasted long), and many of the downtown picture houses, especially the "foreign" theaters located on East Federal Street (the Luna, Luxor, Roma and Napoli), carried a patina of "disrespectability" with many WASPs in the upper classes, who only attended live theater.[21] And yet the moving picture houses grew: the total number had increased to fourteen thousand nationally by the beginning of World War I.[22]

In 1914, the first stable theaters outside of downtown Youngstown emerged. From this date forward, "neighborhood theaters," as they came to be called, spread to every side of the city. The Market Street Theater opened on the south side in September 1914. Capable of seating six hundred people, it became the second-largest theater in the city. The owners, showing the seriousness of the venture, brought in Max Shagrin to manage the new establishment. Max's brother, Joe, worked as the manager of the Grand Opera House, and Max himself eventually moved to California to work for the Warner brothers, whom he met while in Youngstown.

The Wilson Theater also opened in 1914 on Wilson Avenue. Dubbed "A Picture House for the People of the East Side," the new theater catered primarily to families. The Wilson seated four hundred, and its curtain was one of the largest in the area. Films did not show continuously all day, however, as they did in many downtown movie houses. The Wilson was one of the very first theaters in Youngstown to have a large advertisement spread on its opening published in the *Youngstown Vindicator*.

Owner Thomas McVey, a local contractor, built the theater himself. McVey, however, was not familiar with the entertainment business. By 1918,

The former Wilson Theater, located on the east side of Youngstown, is one of the last theater buildings still standing in the Mahoning Valley. *Photo by the author.*

the theater's name had changed to the Wilsonian, and by 1923, it was called the Broadway Theater. Despite such a promising beginning, it had closed by 1929. One workman was killed and another seriously injured in the abandoned structure in October of the same year when the roof above the projection booth caved in.

After years as a residence, it reopened in 1940 as the Wilson Theater, one of three movie houses operating on the east side at the time—including the Home on McGuffey Road and the Lincoln on Himrod Avenue. Carmen J. Leone's "family biography," *Rose Street*, describes trips to the Wilson during its heyday as a haven for east side children: "But most of the movies they saw were at the Wilson, the neighborhood theater, which they walked to with Lena on Saturday afternoons and almost every Monday, Wednesday and Friday, when the movies changed. They plunked down their dimes, which brought them two feature length films, with cartoons, previews and various short subjects sandwiched between."[23]

The year 1914 and the opening of the Wilson marked the transition from an era of the simple downtown nickelodeon to new, more sophisticated theaters. In 1918, the Liberty Theater, the first of the downtown "movie palaces," opened on West Federal Street. In the years that followed, more and more neighborhood theaters spread throughout the city. While Youngstown's theater scene rapidly evolved in the first two decades of the twentieth century, it helped nourish the most famous family to emerge from the city's entertainment world: the Warner family.

THE WARNER BROTHERS IN THE VALLEY

One of the most important families in the history of American cinema arrived in Youngstown, Ohio, in 1896 with almost nothing to their name. The Warners' journey from Baltimore to Youngstown resulted from a trip young Harry Warner took to see William McKinley during his 1896 presidential campaign. Arriving by train in Youngstown, Harry could not help but notice the frantic economic activity in the booming iron city. He soon sent word about this new industrial paradise back to the family in Baltimore.

Ben Warner, the family patriarch, arrived in America years earlier, fleeing anti-Jewish pogroms in Poland, then part of the Russian Empire. His wife, Pearl, ultimately bore twelve children, several of whom died very young—including Cecillia, Henry, Fannie and, later, Milton. Fame, fortune and a fair share of tragedy greeted the Warner clan during their rise to prominence in America, but that is an oft-told tale. Less, however, has been written of the family's impact on local theater culture during their years before finding fame.

Ben Warner's first business in Youngstown was a shoe repair store located near Spring Common. The Baltimore Shoe Repairing Company opened at 340 West Federal Street. Ben offered new shoes for $1.00 and up and handmade shoes for $2.25. Half-sole shoe repairs were $0.50 for men and $0.40 for women.

The Warner family struggled mightily in the new city, living in a ramshackle building at 310 West Federal Street. The girls (Rose, Sadie and Annie) and boys (Albert or "Abe," as he was called; Sam; Harry; Jack; Milton; and David) were all forced to bathe out of the same lead-lined bathtub. Ben commonly fashioned the family's clothes at home, and the children went to work almost as soon as they were able. Despite these difficulties, they stridently maintained a policy of family solidarity—one that eventually helped launch the brothers along a path toward success.

Abe and Milton both excelled at athletics. Abe played standout football as a halfback at Rayen High School, but it was Milton who became the most gifted athlete of the family. He lettered in baseball, track and basketball all while serving as captain of the Rayen football team. Yet Milton's true talent lay with baseball. Able to pitch "like a flame thrower," he received an offer to play with the New York Giants.[24] But in another family tragedy, Milton died from appendicitis in 1915 at the age of nineteen.

Show business was to be the future for Harry, Jack, Sam and Abe. But the brothers took a circuitous route to the film production world. Harry, the oldest, was responsible for bringing the family to Youngstown and played a key role in helping his father run the shoe repair shop. But Harry also pursued a variety of other ventures. The 1890s brought an enormous bicycle craze to America, made possible by new models using chain-driven transmissions. These bicycles, sporting much smaller wheels, attracted the attention of Harry and Abe, who opened Warner Bros. Bicycles at 327 West Federal Street, currently the site of the Tyler Mahoning Valley History Center.

The brothers repaired and rented bicycles at the rate of fifteen cents an hour. Abe also became interested in training and participating in local cycling races. The brothers did business with a variety of well-known bicyclists, including Marshall Taylor, the first African American to become a world champion cyclist. Yet the business floundered, and the brothers moved on to new things. They soon got involved with bowling and opened an alley on Chestnut Street downtown.

An early photo from a fair, somewhere in the Mahoning Valley, shows an advertisement for the film *The Great Train Robbery*, which the Warner brothers screened throughout the local area. *Courtesy of Mahoning Valley Historical Society.*

Around the same time, brother Sam embarked on a similar journey to find his true calling. While at Cedar Point amusement park in Sandusky, he witnessed a showing of Edwin S. Porter's *The Great Train Robbery*, one of the first groundbreaking narrative pictures to use sophisticated editing techniques. Inspired to get involved in show business, Sam leased the Grand Opera House from manager T.K. Albaugh, showing primarily primitive photoplays and vaudeville. The opera house venture did not last long, and Sam soon found himself employed with an outdoor show called "Hale's Tours and Scenes of the World" at Idora Park. The gimmick was to re-create a scenic journey by showing well-known panoramas on film, such as Yosemite National Park, using a touring car, which rocked to simulate motion as customers imagined they were witnessing the scenes firsthand.

When live shows began at the nearby Casino Theater (Idora's live stage theater), concessions closed, including Hale's Tours. Sam met Billy Evans during that time, who later went on to become the youngest umpire in professional baseball, and Harry Burt, the local chocolatier who ran a concession at Idora and who later pioneered the Good Humor ice cream bar.

Sam sampled other occupations, working for the Erie Railroad and selling ice cream cones near a penny arcade on East Federal Street. He eventually met George Olenhauser, later the operator of the Edisona Theater downtown. Olenhauser showed Sam the inner workings of a Kinetoscope Model B camera. Through his connections at Idora Park, Sam and the family learned that an inoperable, but repairable, Kinetoscope was available for sale, yet one problem presented itself: money.

Ben understood and supported his son buying the camera, which included a copy of *The Great Train Robbery*. He agreed to pawn his gold watch and "ol' Bob," the delivery horse from his store, to gather the needed money. (The family later bought Bob back.) The show business bug also bit Harry around the same time. He witnessed the operations of the country's first nickelodeon theater in Pittsburgh. "I looked across the street and could see the nickels rolling in at John P. Harris' Nickelodeon," Harry later said.[25] Equally inspired to try their hand at the new moving picture business, the brothers, camera and film in hand, took their show on the road.

A nearby carnival in Niles, Ohio, attracted the boys' attention. They converted a vacant store into a makeshift theater: a simple sheet served as a screen, and sundry chairs and benches constituted the seating. Rose provided accompaniment on the piano while the jerky film played. *The Great Train Robbery* wound up a huge hit with the audiences of working men and women. It remains unclear where this vacant storefront was in Niles, but the Warners also showed the film at Diebel's Butcher Shop on Mill Street (present-day East State Street). Traveling by rail from town to town, they screened their battered *Great Train Robbery* copy in Girard, Hubbard and Warren, Ohio, as well as in the Pennsylvania cities of Meadville, Sharon and, most famously, New Castle.

The coming of winter cut into the profits and ended their tour of area cities, as unheated storerooms failed to attract many patrons. Lacking a permanent space to show their film, they focused on finding a suitable place for their own theater. Downtown Youngstown lacked affordable storefronts and was home to too many other arcades and nickel theaters. Nearby New Castle, Pennsylvania, however, was one of the fastest-growing cities in the country with few established competitors. New Castle boasted the Genkinger Opera House for live theater, but little else existed in the way of similar entertainment. The Warners quickly rented a storefront and dubbed it the Cascade Theater, named after the city's popular nature and amusement park. On February 2, 1907, they opened the doors for the first time.

Downtown Youngstown as it appeared during the Warner brothers' early years in the city. *Courtesy of the author.*

"It was not a very imposing structure," according to the later remembrances of Jack Warner, "and would not have looked like a theater at all without the gingerbread arch across the entrance, and a phone-booth sized box office....There were a couple of potted palms on either side, whose drooping fronds were tempting targets for the small fry, who yanked at them when no one was around."[26]

Harry, Abe and Sam were forced to borrow chairs from a funeral parlor in order to provide seating (ninety-nine chairs to be exact, just under the limit for a local ordinance that would have forced them to upgrade the theater's fire and safety features). In reality, the Cascade was not dissimilar to the storefront in Niles where they showed *The Great Train Robbery* for the first time. "It was a queer affair," Harry later recalled. "We used a salt-herring barrel filled with wet salt for a rheostat and my brother, Sam, the family projectionist, was continually getting shocked."[27]

The films at the Cascade were so popular that the brothers called in young Jack, then sixteen, to deliberately sing off-key in between shows to scare off customers looking to stay and see the feature again. He also ran errands for the brothers while soaking in the atmosphere of the place. Born in 1892, Jack was the youngest of the brothers, and like the others, he sensed opportunities in the new world of moving pictures.

As with his brothers, Jack held a variety of jobs. He worked as a delivery boy for his father and as a newsboy for the *Youngstown Vindicator*. He once slept all night in the newsroom to get the first "extra" election editions hot off the press.[28] At a young age, he began visiting Banner Studio, located at 16 West Federal Street in Youngstown. Banner specialized in photographic portraiture: a customer could get their photo processed for a penny while they waited or five different portraits with different poses for a quarter. Jack spent so much time at Banner that the manager began using him as a subject for test photos. "That Warner kid was a pest," studio owner Pat Stanton later said.[29] While hanging around Banner, Jack became inspired by photographer Eadweard Muybridge's studies of a galloping horse caught in motion; it was his first introduction to film.

Jack dropped out of school before he could make it to Rayen; instead, he tried to become a star in the world of vaudeville. After Ben Warner left the shoe business, he opened a market with an attached soda fountain on East Federal Street in downtown Youngstown. There, Jack met one of his father's employees, a south side girl, Rae Samuels. In later years, she became famous as the "Blue Streak of Vaudeville," commanding nearly $1,500 a week as a traveling star. Samuels recognized Jack's singing talent and encouraged him to get voice lessons and assume a stage name. The duo invented the name "Leon Zuardo," which Jack used while performing in Youngstown and during a one-year tour on the vaudeville circuit.

Locally, Jack performed with the stock company Wright Huntington and His Players. He eventually came to the attention of theater owners Emil Renner (of the Renner Brewery family) and C.W. Deibel, who later opened the Liberty Theater. In 1906, Renner and Deibel opened the first Dome Theater in a vacant storefront at 206 West Federal Street. After hearing about Jack's singing, they offered him eighteen dollars a week to serenade crowds at the Dome. He later recalled the experience:

> *I came on between nickelodeon shows, and it was some time before I realized that I was sort of a reverse shill. My act gave the ushers time to nudge people out of the theater—there were only 180 seats—and make room for the next group lining up outside. Dibble [sic] and Renner theorized that only a stubborn customer would hang around to listen to a boy soprano, but in actual practice I had a group of devoted fans who stayed in their seats until I finished my act.[30]*

Jack's performance career did not last long. Though he was still young, he soon realized that the money in show business was behind the scenes.

The Warner brothers sold the Cascade Theater ten months after young Jack first arrived to sing. Despite the theater's success, they lacked a steady

Jack Warner sang in between shows at the original Dome Theater. Warner Brothers later took an interest in the movie house. *Courtesy of Mahoning Valley Historical Society.*

stream of new films. The boys quickly moved into film distribution. The Duquesne Amusement and Supply Company (sometimes credited as the first of its kind), headquartered outside of Pittsburgh, leased movies to a growing number of theaters hungry for new films. It even published its own monthly magazine, the *Duquesne Film Noise*. Yet the Warners eventually fell afoul of Thomas Edison and his Edison Trust, a monopolistic organization seeking patent protection for Edison's film equipment, which was widely used. Edison's organization essentially took over distribution in the country by using the General Film Company to buy out or marginalize independent film exchanges like the Warners' Duquesne Company.

Driven out of the distribution business, the boys regrouped. Harry helped open the Rex Theater downtown in 1911, the first theater in Youngstown the Warners held a stake in. Located at 135 West Federal Street, *Moving Picture World* referred to it as "the first and foremost theater" in the city at the time.[31] The theater entrance featured tiles emblazoned with a crown and the Rex name. White marble was featured throughout. The theater could seat 299—once again, a nod to the taxation rule. A six-piece orchestra provided accompaniment for the films, shown on an elegant screen.

David M. Robins, a member of the famous Robins Theater family in Warren and Niles, co-owned the Rex. David had married Annie Warner years earlier at Diamond Hall in downtown Youngstown. Jack Warner Jr. later remembered Robins as "a hulking person who seldom had anything to say. I see him plainly in my mind, but it is a silent picture which fades as fast as it appears. He seems to have a done good job, because I rarely heard my father say anything about him, which was not true when he spoke of his other brothers-in-law."[32] Robins went on to manage the Dome Theater after Warner Brothers obtained control of it, and later, he became the first manager of the Warner Theater in Youngstown.

After the leftover films from the old Duquesne Company ran out, Harry sold his stake in the Rex Theater. But it did not end the Warners' relationship with Youngstown and Mahoning Valley. During World War I, the brothers began producing their own films. In 1918, after their first major hit, *My Four Years in Germany*, they opened a Hollywood studio with Jack and Sam as dual heads of production. By 1924, Warner Brothers Pictures was surviving due to the popularity of films featuring the dog Rin Tin Tin and *The Marriage Circle*, the studio's biggest hit that year. Meanwhile, in Youngstown, Warner Brothers acquired the Dome Theater, a rebuilt and enlarged version of the old theater where a young Jack Warner once sang.

The old Dome was enlarged in 1908 to seat 299. In 1912, Renner and Deibel reopened the new structure and expanded it to 800 seats. Another expansion in 1915 increased seating to 1,100. The new Dome was the first large theater in Youngstown dedicated solely to motion pictures. The Dome's management originally contracted to show Fox and Paramount Pictures films. After Warner Brothers took control, Warner son-in-law David Robins became treasurer and later manager.

With Warner Brothers Pictures still a struggling studio, Sam worked toward bringing the world of sound to silent cinema. Without much support from his brothers, Sam became fascinated with the idea of talking pictures when he discovered the Western Electric sound-on-disk system. After much prodding, he convinced the brothers to back a system to develop sound pictures with Western Electric. The new system, dubbed "Vitaphone," premiered with the Warner's picture *Don Juan*, a film with a soundtrack but no spoken dialogue. The Dome made Youngstown the third city in the country, after New York and Chicago, to feature Vitaphone.[33] The next test hurdle was to bring sound to motion picture dialogue.

Youngstown theater manager Jack Hynes, who worked at the Dome, related Abe Warner's feelings about developing "talkies" after a conversation he had with him shortly before the debut of their first "talkie," *The Jazz Singer*: "I remember a very funny thing he said to us that day. He said, if it wasn't successful, 'We are liable to come back to Youngstown and open pa's butcher shop and start over again.'"[34]

The Jazz Singer stunned audiences, and though not entirely apparent at the time, it signaled the beginning of the end of silent film. All of this proved to be bittersweet for the Warner brothers, however. Sam, in yet one more family tragedy, died of pneumonia a day before the premiere of the film.

Sam Warner was the driving force behind Warner Brothers' pioneering of "talkies" in the late 1920s. *Courtesy of Mahoning Valley Historical Society.*

None of the Warner brothers were present on the night of October 6, 1927, for the opening in New York City. Yet the film's success, and the eventual triumph of talkies, served as a lasting memorial to Sam Warner's vision.

Through it all, parents Ben and Pearl Warner remained in Mahoning Valley. For years, Ben operated a store in downtown Youngstown, eventually moving his operation to 536 Poland Avenue. After relocating to 501 Belmont Avenue and then to Smoky Hollow, where he ran a store on North Watt Street, Ben and Pearl settled near the corner of Elm Street and Bissell Avenue on the city's north side. In an interesting twist, Ben himself eventually moved into show business in Niles, where the brothers first exhibited their copy of *The Great Train Robbery* years earlier.

The theater Ben Warner came to run started its life as the Verbeck Theater. The George H. Verbeck Company built Niles's first theater in December 1903. The first real venue of its kind in the growing steel town attracted enormous interest, with some seats on opening night going for as much as ten dollars. In 1911, it was sold and became known as the Grand Opera House.

While his sons were trying to open their Hollywood studio, Ben became the manager of the opera house. Ben and daughter Sadie lived at 16 West Church Street in 1916, a year after Ben became manager and a year before Sadie married Ben's assistant manager, Louis Halper. According to the *Youngstown Vindicator*, "Warner for many years was a familiar figure on the streets of Niles, spending much of his time on the sidewalk in front of the theater pleasantly greeting passerby or chattering with acquaintances."[35]

In September 1920, a film exploded at the opera house, sparking a fire that spread throughout the theater. After the near destruction of the old opera house, Ben announced the building of a Warner Theater in its place for an estimated $100,000. The new Warner opened in 1921, a full decade before the Youngstown Warner Theater. Ben obtained a $15,000 organ and had the gutted third floor of the building removed. The new structure, designed by Stanley and Scheible of Youngstown, featured an enlarged auditorium without a balcony, unlike the old Grand Opera. A firewall was placed around the projector room to prevent a repeat of the 1920 blaze. In 1923, Ben and Pearl moved into an apartment above the theater.

The new Warner became the gem of Niles, a sign of the industrial city's prominence in Mahoning Valley. For those children who could not afford the admission, Pearl often looked the other way and let them in to enjoy a show. Ben held free movie nights for the *Niles Times*'s newsboys.

"DAD" AND "MA" WARNER CELEBRATE GOLDEN ANNIVERSARY

THE GOLDEN
WEDDING DAY
August 4th, 1876—August 24th, 1926.

Harry and Abe and Sam and Jack,
All of 'em hitting the home track,
All hell-bent to keep a date
With Dad and Mom in the Buckeye State—
And Dave and Sadye and Anna and Rose,
Hurrying swift as the wind that blows,
Hurrying back where they started from—
Back to the old town and Dad and Mom.

Dad and Mom for these fifty years,
Have shared life's trials, hopes and fears
And now the children who've learned to roam,
Are hurrying, scurrying, flurrying home,
How Dad and Mom will gloat to see
All of 'em home, like they used to be.

For there's one gift that's far above
All other gifts; we call it—Love;
It's like the answer to every prayer;
To know, when old, that the children care.
Rose, Anna and Sadye—Dave and Jack—
Abe and Harry—are taking Love back;
All eager to give, in their own good way,
Their Love—on the Golden Wedding Day

MA WARNER   DAD WARNER

ROSE

SADYE   ANNA

HARRY   ALBERT

DAVE

JACK   SAM

The Golden Wedding of Mr. and Mrs. Benjamin Warner was celebrated in the old home town, Youngstown, Ohio, on the evening of August 25th, 1926. All the boys were there, Harry, Abe, Sam, Jack! All the
wives were there and the children! All the best of the old friends and the best of the new! The hardships of
the half-century had faded out! Happiness had faded in! It was a glorious scene! Sun up! Not like afternoon at all! Like morning! New fires lit! Old fires rekindled! A re-awakening of everything! A re-blos-
soming! A scene that might have been aptly titled: "Came the Dawn!"
       That friendly old hostelry, "The Ohio Hotel," was the scene of fore-gathering. About the board were
fifty guests, one for each year of the gallant pilgrimage. The Young Couple sat at the head of the table, all
a-flutter with the magic of it all! In and out rushed diminutive bell-boys, bearing telegrams of congratulation
from the Four Quarters of the Globe, and the Seven Seas, too, it seemed!
       Then came the tender ebb and flow of the old-time music, the dash and crash of the new! And the
dancing! Then the well-wishing! And the good nights. And at last the Bride and Groom, radiant, grateful,
young-of-heart, arm in arm, climbing the stairs, together!
       To such as these all days are Golden Wedding Days!

Ben and Pearl Warner's golden wedding anniversary was held at the Hotel Pick-Ohio in
1926. It was the last time the whole family gathered together; Sam Warner died the next
year. *Courtesy of Mahoning Valley Historical Society.*

"Dad," as the locals sometimes called Warner, remained a beloved figure even after divesting himself of the theater, which was taken over by Robins Enterprises in 1927.

The year before the Robins group took over the Warner Theater, the Warner boys returned to Youngstown for Ben and Pearl's golden wedding anniversary in August 1926. Fifty family members fêted the couple at the Hotel Pick-Ohio downtown. For a moment, it seemed like old times, but it would be the last time the entire family would be together; Sam died a year later. Pearl and Ben eventually moved to California to be closer to their children. In 1935, while visiting Annie and David Robins at their north side home, Ben died. The next day, all of Youngstown's theaters halted their showings for two minutes in honor of Ben Warner, father of the most famous brothers in motion pictures.

No members of the Warner family live in the area today; however, their legacy lives on in Powers Auditorium, the former Warner Theater in Youngstown, built to honor the late Sam Warner. The story of the Warner boys' rise from rags to riches has long since become legend, but the history of the Warners and their start in Mahoning Valley also lives on in the annals of film history, reminding us of a time when the Steel Valley helped birth a Hollywood dynasty.

Part 2

A BAWDY BURLESQUE TOWN

A Town Where You Can Take It All Off

You can show everything in Youngstown.
—June Allen, burlesque dancer, 1950

From the late 1940s to the late 1960s, a corner of South Champion Street in downtown Youngstown served as a haven for young men, the curious, thrill seekers and those who appreciated the sight of the female form gyrating to the music of a brass brand. Depending on whom you asked, the Park Burlesque was either a local institution or a local eyesore. Careful mothers knew not to walk their children near the side of the theater building featuring posters and advertisements of the scantily clad stars of the Park stage. A connoisseur would recognize the faces of starlets such as Virginia Bell or Georgia Sothern walking from the Tod Hotel to the Brass Rail and on to the Park for a night's performance. The Park was the most well known of Youngstown's various burlesque houses over the years. A working-class city par excellence, Youngstown embraced the working-class art form of burlesque, and the Princess, Grand, Strand, Park and New Park Burlesk gave the city a reputation as a place that appreciated the risqué.

The art form burlesque evolved from the world of vaudeville. Skits, song and dance routines, minstrel shows, numbers with animals and more made up the always-varied vaudeville bills that played on the stages of the nineteenth and twentieth centuries. From these shows came musical variety numbers featuring lurid humor and female dancers—often in what was considered revealing clothing. By today's standards, however, it was all fairly tame. At the Grand Opera House in the 1880s, audiences went wild over dancers performing the can-can. The city had never seen anything like it. Youngstown's first burlesque show premiered a decade later at the same venue.

"Lurid posters featuring buxom, red-cheeked women with well-turned calves peeping from beneath fluffy, ruffled skirts, adorned the front of the theater," according to Joe Shagrin, a young newsboy at the time.[36] The main show that night in 1898 featured the "Great Rubie," who performed a partial striptease while riding a bicycle. But this early performance paled in comparison to the routines that became commonplace decades later at the Grand Theater and the Park Burlesque. Burlesque at the time was just beginning its evolution.

With dancing girls and off-color comedians, the heart of burlesque during its golden age from the 1920s to the 1940s represented only a part of the vaudeville world. The term *burlesque* originally denoted a performance that was a humorous parody or sendup of something else. That all changed in the 1920s as vaudeville began its decline and motion pictures began to dominate the world of entertainment. "Burlesque was essentially a vaudeville show with strippers," historian Nat Bodian argued.[37] Some theaters featuring vaudeville became full-time burlesque houses, complete with striptease dancing, in order to survive the competition from movie theaters. The Princess Theater became the first in Youngstown to go that route.

The Princess Theater

The Princess, known as the "Pretty Theater with a Pretty Name," opened in 1908 on South Champion Street during a time when live theater still held sway. Along with the Park Theater and the Grand Opera House, it was among the finest show houses in Mahoning Valley. The Princess initially ran a "vaudeville-only" program—three shows a day with admission rates from ten to twenty-five cents, based on reserve seating. Owners Seas and Young also controlled the Princess establishments in Cleveland, Columbus and Cambridge and hoped that their new venture would tap into the rapidly growing Youngstown theater scene. Yet only four years after opening, the

The Princess Theater evolved from a vaudeville house to a burlesque house, Youngstown's first, in the 1930s. *Courtesy of Mahoning Valley Historical Society.*

Princess, under new management, began to move away from an all-vaudeville format.

Motion pictures began to supplement the usual variety bills, and management purchased several state-of-the-art projectors for the house. Family-friendly films and pictures portraying social issues screened, usually after a minstrel or variety show; during the 1920s, the Princess was also billed as the "Family Theater." Management control eventually passed into the hands of Ralph Pitzer, a veteran of the theater scene and an early confidant of the Warner brothers. Vaudeville and live performances still dominated the theater's offerings during much of Pitzer's time at the Princess. Bob Hope, Jack Benny and Red Skelton (who played for thirty-one dollars a week in 1931) all appeared on its stage. The house was eventually enlarged from a maximum seating capacity of 430 to about 800.

In 1927, Emil Renner, an original owner of the Dome Theater, and some local investors purchased the Princess with the goal of turning it into the city's leading vaudeville house. By the early 1930s, though, vaudeville was barely clinging to life as a popular art form. Looking for a way to save the Princess, burlesque took center stage, and around late 1934, the theater became a full-time burlesque house. Dancers such as Sonya-Lee (the "Sophisticated Lady") and Chickee Wells (the "China Doll") began gracing the stage of the Princess. On Mother's Day, the ladies at the Princess performed a dance in honor of moms, complete with a chorus line. During the height of the Depression, lonely and down-and-out men could be counted on to find enough change to buy a brief escape into the world of the burlesque ladies.

Not everyone held the Princess in high esteem, however. Local columnist Esther Hamilton attended a show for one of her columns. She was none too impressed: "It was all very amateurish. It reminded me of an amateur play of my high school days." William Peyko described a trip he took to the Princess as a young man in much more plain language: "There was a guy with a trumpet and a few other people in the [orchestra] pit by the stage.

They'd play for the girls. The women that they had there, hell, they were old. They were dancing and chewing gum! The M.C. would introduce them: 'now the lovely ladies are gonna dance for you!'" Still, the Princess, and indeed the entire world of burlesque, began attracting unwanted attention from "reformist" mayors and eager vice squads as the Depression wore on.

In the mid-1930s, the newly elected mayor of New York City, Fiorello La Guardia, launched a war against organized crime in the city. He followed up his pursuit of the Big Apple's gangsters with an effort to shut down the city's numerous burlesque houses. Mayor Lionel Evans took a similar approach in Youngstown, unleashing Police Chief Carl Olson on the Princess in 1937. Within a short period of time, the police department cleared the Princess of all external advertising and issued a warning that the theater would be shut down completely upon any reports of "stripping." But economic hard times, not community standards, ultimately put an end to the Princess, and the theater unceremoniously closed in 1939. The "Pretty Theater with a Pretty Name" ended its life known as the "Gaudy Lady."

The Grand Burlesk

Burlesque in the city nonetheless took on a life of its own, and the old Princess became the Grand Theater—or the Grand Burlesk, as it was often called—a notorious establishment that pushed the bounds of propriety far more than the "Gaudy Lady" ever did. Many famous comedians and performers such as Al Jolson began their careers working burlesque, and local up-and-coming comedians worked the Grand in the same spirit. Comics, "straight men" and "baggy pants" comedians all proved integral to the humorous aspect of burlesque shows—warming up the crowds for the lovely ladies. All of this culminated with the headliner for the night, often an established star on the circuit.

The Grand engaged a variety of shows, including "black and white revues" starring both white and black dancers like the Harlem Hotshots. But the Grand remained too small to bring in the biggest stars, although Vicki Wells, a top draw on the burlesque circuit during the 1940s, played the Grand twice in 1946. On her rise to fame, burlesque star Gypsy Rose Lee played the much larger Palace Theater when in town.

World War II not only boosted the economy, but it also buoyed the burlesque houses as well. "Oriental Nights," featuring twelve dancing "Oriental maidens," packed in crowds at the Grand as America prepared for war. In 1942, the theater closed early for summer after a police investigation was launched over the so-called hot shows at the Grand. But the shows went on. The famous Gladys Fox graced the stage in 1943. New Year's Eve programs during the war typically lasted until dawn, giving audiences plenty of time to ogle Sen Lee Fu (the "Oriental dream girl" with "more curves than the Burma Road") and Rosita and her 1943 Follies. At a show in New York, when dancer June Allen found her tassel dance censored, she lamented that the Big Apple was not more like the Steel City: "Give me a place like Youngstown," Allen said. "You can show everything in Youngstown, and yet I don't think the people there are more immoral than anywhere else."[38]

The Park Burlesque

While the Grand across the street attracted a certain audience, the Park Theater—long one of Mahoning Valley's most respected live theaters—faced a crisis in 1948. The Park opened to the public as a stage theater in 1901. It could seat 1,638, putting it on par with the Grand Opera House in size. The dazzling interior included a sumptuous proscenium arch (containing both plaster and marble) and box seats (in cream and gold) covered by a beaded glass dome lit from above. The dome produced an effect akin to a sky at night with the moon overhead. Smoking rooms, marble drinking fountains and classical columns gave the impression of a grand theater of the highest order. "Built by Youngstown people for Youngstown," the Park quickly became a Mahoning Valley institution and one of the largest theaters in northeast Ohio.[39] Over the years, the Park attracted top talent: Cecil B. DeMille (starring in a comedy), Helen Hayes, John Kenley (of Kenley Players fame), Ethel Barrymore, Al Jolson, Joe E. Lewis and Katharine Hepburn, among others. Harry Houdini even performed one of his spellbinding magic acts at the theater.

As motion pictures began to overpower live productions, the Park began to show films. Famed local managers Joe Shagrin (who worked under George M. Cohan, then owner) and Jack Hynes guided the theater during its glory years. And as late as 1948, the Park remained a local institution. That same year, disaster struck when a grid in the theater's stage cracked during a live showing of *Oklahoma!* Faced with an inability to pay the massive expenses required to fix the stage, the owners leased the theater to J.O. Kane, operator of the Grand Theater. Kane transferred the Grand to the old Park building and rechristened it the Park Burlesque.

The Grand's former building, originally built as the Princess, became the Esquire Theater before it was eventually demolished in 1954.

Much to the consternation of some in the city, including newly elected mayor Charles Henderson, the Park Burlesque opened in November 1948. The old Park building proved to be ideal for the new burlesque house. Many of the top stars and circuits required larger venues, and the Park building far outsized the old Grand/Princess venue; the new Park could now handle continuous performances common to that era.

Opening night, the great Vicki Wells returned to the city for a stellar show. Burlesque in Youngstown was hitting the big time. The Park became a stop on the eastern part of the burlesque circuit, which covered eighteen larger and midsized cites on the coast and in Youngstown, Dayton and Columbus. The theater continued the Grand's tradition of boisterous New Year's Eve shows in 1948—inviting guys and gals from "eighteen to eighty." The festivities ran all night long from seven o'clock to five o'clock in the morning; anyone could drop in at any time during the continuous show.

The Park, like the Grand before it, featured a fair number of ethnic dancers, billed as "exotic" attractions, who usually played on stereotypes of the day. Amy Fong, star of a revue called *China Dolls*, appeared in 1949. Touted as an "authentic" Asian, Fong often wore part of a traditional Chinese dress with a G-string—considered enormously scandalous by the standards of

For two decades, the Park Burlesque brought the finest comedians and dancers to the Mahoning Valley. *Courtesy of Mahoning Valley Historical Society.*

traditional Chinese society.[40] World War II increased the presence of African American women on the burlesque circuit. The Harlem Hotshots starred at both the Grand and at the Park, along with "Dusty Freeman's Harlem on Parade." Often relegated to minor roles in films, black women found the world of burlesque more amenable. As with Asian women, they were billed as specific acts: "colored," exotic, high brown and so on.[41]

Probably the most well-known act at the Park in the 1940s and 1950s was the illustrious Rose La Rose, the first woman to earn $2,000 per week performing on the circuit. Often called the "Queen of Burlesque," Rose obtained her stage name after a sign painter, deeming her given name of Rosina DePella too tame, changed it to the soon-to-be-famous sobriquet. Known for pushing the envelope on stage, she once appeared at the Park performing a tune called "I Love You, Daddy." She wore only an electric heart over her G-sting during the show, and when she hit a button on a chord attached to it, the heart lit up, much to the audience's delight.

In the late 1940s, Rose performed in Youngstown to a classical score of the "William Tell Overture" and "Clair de Lune." "All burlesque stars have gimmicks," she told the Youngstown press. "Gypsy Rose Lee writes novels—wonderful gimmick. Sally Rand lectures—she knows all about fans. With me, it's music." When local classical music fans denounced her use of the pieces, she called them out: "Opera audiences are hypocrites....Half of them don't understand good music or even like it, but they go to the opera because they want people to think they are cultured. Whereas people who come to see me like what they are going to see, and believe me, they understand it. Especially the music."[42]

The *Youngstown Vindicator* sarcastically responded to Rose's comments, asking that "teachers and others who have been worried about the public outlook toward the classics not be discouraged. The turnout for Miss La Rose at the Park over the weekend definitely indicated a revival of interest in music since a large percentage of the audience were women."[43] Few paid the paper much mind, and Rose became the era's top box office draw locally.

Rose eventually obtained her own place in 1958, Toledo's Town Hall Theater. After the Town Hall fell during urban renewal in 1968, she bought the Esquire Theater down the road. Mentoring young women in the profession until her untimely death in 1972 at the age of fifty-three, Rose steadfastly defended burlesque. "Burlesque is more than just girls stripping," she said. "It is beautiful costumes, comics, production numbers, and much more."[44]

Right: Rose La Rose was the Park's most popular draw during the late 1940s and 1950s. She later opened her own burlesque house in Toledo, Ohio. *Courtesy of the author*.

Below: The Park attracted its fair share of controversy over the years but remained a rite of passage for many young men in Youngstown. *Courtesy of Mahoning Valley Historical Society*.

If Rose La Rose frequently courted controversy, then so did the Park, whether intentionally or not. In 1948, voters elected Republican Charles Henderson as mayor. A reformist candidate, Henderson took on organized crime locally, appointing the tireless Edward Allen as his chief of police. Soon the local world of burlesque attracted the administration's attention, and Allen placed tight regulations on the Park. He employed undercover agents to report on any shows that might go "too far." The Park's management reacted vociferously, complaining that the regulations required dancers to "retain too much clothing," thus hurting attendance.[45] After the Henderson administration exited office, things seemed to calm down, but it was short-lived.

The Park became the headquarters for the eastern circuit of burlesque theaters for the 1957–58 season. Accordingly, shows began in Youngstown before traveling throughout Ohio and the Eastern Seaboard. Dancers and comedians on the circuit usually worked eighteen-week stretches, continuously traveling. The Park's newfound importance in the burlesque world once again attracted the unwanted attention of local law enforcement. Complaints about the shows reached the police after a newspaper reporter called about a particular star stripping down to nothing but a mink stole. After a brief crackdown, the Park continued as usual. However, by the late 1950s, the authorities had focused their attention on preventing another former movie theater from becoming a burlesque house: the Strand.

The Strand Theater

The Strand "on the Square" opened in 1916 along with the new Tod Hotel downtown. The same architects responsible for the Hippodrome Theater on West Federal Street situated it on the northeast part of the Tod building. The new show house could seat more than one thousand, placing it just behind the Park, Hippodrome and the Grand Opera House in size. A barrel-vaulted ceiling in gold, ivory and marble greeted patrons near the entrance of the theater, which led to the main-floor seating area, balcony and box seats. Silent film star Rose Tapley appeared to greet the public at the Strand in 1917. In the 1920s, John P. Harris, who with others was later responsible for creating the Ice Capades, managed the theater, and Jack Hynes started his career working at the Strand.

The Strand showed second-run features (films that had finished a thirty-day run elsewhere). In the 1920s, the theater often featured seven different

The Strand Theater converted to an all-burlesque format in the late 1950s, much to the chagrin of Youngstown's city fathers. *Courtesy of Thomas Molocea.*

films a week. The Strand, unlike the Dome and the Hippodrome, survived the Great Depression and even received a major renovation in 1939. It began a slow decline after World War II, one that put the theater at pains to survive by the 1950s. Saturday morning serials, live country music shows, rockabilly and singing acts featuring such stars as Youngstown's own Dorisetta Clark and Nat King Cole kept the books in the black. But with the theater's fortunes still in doubt, management decided to change to an all-burlesque format.

The timing was unfortunate. In June 1958, Mayor Frank X. Kryzan asked the city council to pass legislation banning any "lascivious and immoral exhibitions" within the city. To erase any doubts as to whether or not he considered the girlie shows to be part of a proposed ban, Kryzan declared that Youngstown would be a better city without the presence of burlesque.[46] Management at the Strand attempted to reopen the theater for burlesque less than a month later. While waiting for the council's resolution, the mayor, horrified that a burlesque house might open on Central Square, used the city's building codes to prevent the Strand reopening. Building inspectors declared that the lack of restrooms for performers and inadequate changing rooms prevented the Strand from hosting burlesque shows, even though the theater had already been showing live music performances. Management, surprising the city, readily agreed to upgrade the facilities; this ended any leverage the city might have had over the Strand.

In August 1958, the first burlesque show was staged—complete with a phalanx of officers from the Morality Squad. Aggrieved young men in the audience joked that the proceedings were all too tame, probably as a result of police pressure. However, the new Strand continued to operate. "It is doubtful if any other city has a burlesque house in the town square," a *Youngstown Vindicator* editorial entitled "Decadence in Central Square" complained at the time. "Very few cities have one burlesque house, let alone two, and it's extremely doubtful if this cheap, bawdy entertainment is exhibited so prominently anywhere else as it is in Youngstown's Central Square."[47] Still, the show went on.

Management brought in the likes of Rita Grable ("Burlesque's Bounciest Blonde") and the ever-popular Virginia Bell. The shows usually ran from noon until midnight, with special late-night shows until the early morning hours on the weekend. The Strand added odd combinations of films and dancing, which included a double-feature documentary on the Nazis followed by the "Strip-a-Rama" live stage show. Youngstown became one of the few cities of its size with two burlesque houses in the immediate downtown area. Yet the girlie shows did not save the Strand Theater, which closed for good in 1960.

The Park Becomes the "New" Park

The heat remained on the Park as well. In 1960, after a season so profitable that the theater remained open until May (the Park normally closed a few months during the summer), city officials contemplated padlocking the building after the Youngstown Police Department's Morality Squad determined that at least one show had "exceeded the bounds of decency."[48] But the Park not only survived, it thrived. After four new cities were added to the Park's circuit in late 1960, longer shows and a longer season ensued.

The Park Burlesque during the 1960s remained a rite of passage for young men and a favorite hangout for many not-so-young men. "I had an uncle once who tried to give me some advice," Joe Tronzo reminisced. "'Joe, never go to a burlesque show; you'll see something you're not supposed to see'….When I was in junior high school, a gang of us went to the Park Theater in Youngstown….I saw something I shouldn't have seen: I saw my uncle."[49] During the 1960s, the underage or the barely of age sat in the Park's darkened auditorium alongside the steelworkers, prominent community members and the infamous men with their hats in their laps— all observing a Youngstown tradition.

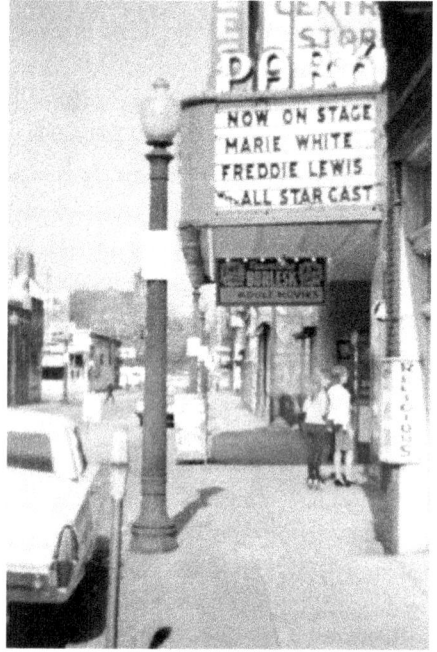

Right: Urban renewal condemned the old Park Theater in 1968; the New Park Burlesk on West Federal Street replaced it. *Courtesy of Mahoning Valley Historical Society.*

Below: The Park's stage is still visible as crews demolish the old burlesque house in 1968. *Courtesy of Mahoning Valley Historical Society.*

The tradition eventually ended in the late 1960s. Planners had targeted much of the east end of downtown for urban renewal, an ominous sign for the Park's future. In 1967, the city, using eminent domain, purchased the Park and adjacent properties on South Champion Street. In January 1968, the city agreed to buy all of the fixtures and furnishings in the Park and continue the theater's lease until April. Demolition crews descended on the building that summer, blasting through sixty-seven years of history. As they pulled the building down and the interior of the theater became visible, pedestrians could still see the sign by the stage that read, "Meet the Guys and Dolls Backstage."

As the grand beauty of the east end fell, plans were in place to build a new Park Theater. In late 1968, construction began on the "New" Park Burlesk, situated on the site of the former Earle Hotel on West Federal Street. In an interesting historical what-if, the Park almost relocated to the old Warner Theater building.[50] The fact that a new theater was built at all proved noteworthy—only two new burlesque houses had opened across the country in the previous five years.[51]

The New Park proved to be quite different from the old in several ways. The building could only seat 360, and the interior featured none of the grand architectural detail of the South Champion building. "It was just a large room," according to Bob Vargo. "They built a large room with a platform at one end, the strippers came out, and that was it, period." The theater's policy also incorporated adult films as a major part of the programming; movies were screened during the day, with dancing in the evening.

One of the New Park's main attractions was Sandra "Busty Russell" Churchey. Called the "Eighth Wonder of the World" and "Miss 56," among others, Russell, with the possible exception of Rose La Rose, is the most fondly remembered locally. Billed with the measurements 50-26-36, she played the old Park as early as 1962, one year before being arrested at the Victory Theater in Toronto, Canada, for giving an "indecent performance." "All she was wearing was a flesh colored G-string and two sequined butterflies," a local detective complained.[52] But despite the arrest, Russell became a headliner in many burlesque houses across the country, particularly in Pennsylvania and Ohio. In addition to the Park, she appeared regularly at the State Theater in Canton, Ohio.

In 1972, police arrested Russell at the Palace Theater on Market Street for "nudism." By this time, burlesque as an art form was on its way out, and theaters—often showing adult films as the main attraction—moved away from the traditional bawdy shows of old. In a 1978 interview, Russell, still performing, lamented the passing of traditional burlesque in the world of the 1970s: "The Good Old days of burlesque really were the good old days," Russell said. "Strippers were really stars back then. I was even interviewed by the Saturday Evening Post in 1962….It was a real show back then. Today it's completely different. I'm not crazy about the way it's turned."[53]

Burlesque historian Leslie Zemeckis argued that burlesque devolved into something very different: "For many boys, what had become a rite of passage, sneaking into theaters to experience their first glimpse of naked flesh, was quickly replaced with X-rated films and gentleman's strip clubs, where there was little to take off. It was full-throttle nudity." By the 1970s, those changes were seen at the New Park as well, which increasingly advertised itself as an adult theater as the decade progressed.

Life for the musicians of burlesque changed, too. Frank "Big Daddy" Delio graduated from the esteemed Berklee College of Music in 1951. Delio performed all across the country with numerous acts, including a gig with Guy Lombardo, but he found steady employment as an organ player in the orchestra pit at the Park Burlesque. Delio eventually worked his way up to become bandleader. "I used to write music for all the girls, the dancers," Delio said.

Not long after transferring to the New Park on West Federal Street, he found himself among the last live musicians playing at the theater. Times were changing. Two years after stagehands were eliminated, management dismissed the last members of the orchestra. "When I started playing at the [Park] Burlesque, we'd have seven guys in the pit," Delio recalled. "In 1971, they started bringing in more comedians, and they let the band go. My drummer and I were the last two to play live burlesque in this town. All the burlesque [music] went to tapes."

The New Park's management also began hosting frequent "amateur nights" to avoid paying union dues to dancers. In 1974, the theater tried another gimmick—bringing in Francesca "Kitten" Natividad, Miss Nude Universe and former Russ Meyer actress, to lead a parade down West Federal Street. The cost-cutting measures and gimmicks seemed to work for a while, but rumors of organized crime involvement and strange happenings circulated around the theater. In 1976, the Park's manager, William Tackett, informed police that he had been the target of an extortion attempt and that someone had sliced off his dog's ear and sent it to him at the theater.

In early 1979, a fire broke out at the theater, causing an estimated $100,000 in damages. Several employees accused a disgruntled dancer of having started the fire over back pay owed to her. Almost one year

Welcome To The

PARK THEATRE

Open Daily from 12 Noon to 12 Midnight

Live Shows at 2, 5, 8 and 11 p.m.

Fri. and Sat., Late Show at 1 p.m.

446 W. FEDERAL STREET
YOUNGSTOWN, OHIO 44502
PHONE 744-5407

Every Monday two or three New Features and three First Run XXX Rated Movies.

We also recommend you visit the Stage Door Lounge next to the theater, where there is continuous entertainment. From 7:00 p.m. to 2:00 a.m. Open daily 11:00 a.m. 'til 2:30 a.m.

To continue to bring you the finest in Entertainment Admission can vary weekly.

Watch for our AMATEUR NIGHT - Check our schedule of dates.

Coming Attractions

September 25th
LYDIA LOVE .... Star. Adm. $7.00

October 2nd
RITA ATLANTA .... Star. Adm. $7.00

October 6th and 7th
AMATEUR NIGHT .... Star. Adm. $7.00

October 9th
RUSTY RUSSEL .... Star. Adm. $7.00

October 16th
LINDA BRIDGETTE ...... Star. Adm. $6.00

October 20th & 21st
AMATEUR NIGHT .... Star. Adm. $7.00

October 23rd
JESSICA JAMES .... Star. Adm. $6.00

October 30th
BABETTE BARDOT ...... Star. Adm $7.00

November 3rd & 4th
AMATEUR NIGHT .... ..Star. Adm. $7.00

We reserve the right to change the schedule without notice.

— ASK FOR GROUP RATES —

A program from the New Park Burlesk advertises upcoming shows, including amateur night. *Courtesy of the author.*

later, another fire (this time catastrophic) thoroughly destroyed the Park's interior and brought down the roof. The manager was later charged with arson. The Park subsequently closed, and the rebuilt structure became a plasma center in 1993.

The burlesque shows and the Park Theater have long since passed from the scene. The Tod Hotel and Hotel Pick-Ohio, themselves long gone, no longer host the lovely ladies of the bawdy shows. No more young men venture to the Park for a day of forbidden fun. Yet the memory of Youngstown's storied burlesque history lives on, still dancing through the minds of many men who grew up in the Steel City.

Part 3

NEIGHBORHOOD THEATERS
IN THE VALLEY

CAMPBELL, STRUTHERS AND CANFIELD

Nickelodeons first appeared in downtown Youngstown, and within several years they had spread to neighborhoods throughout the city and the surrounding industrial suburbs. The moving picture house ceased to be an attraction solely based in the central business district. Neighborhood theaters, usually smaller and more intimate than their downtown counterparts, served neighborhoods where children and families could go to enjoy a show without the need for a trolley trip to Federal Street in the business district.

The industrial suburbs of Campbell and Struthers—along with the largely rural suburb of Canfield—proved to be no exceptions. These communities housed one or several theaters at various times, and these local picture houses, though gone for many years now, etched themselves into the minds of many who grew up in their auditoriums watching serials like *Flash Gordon*, Three Stooges films and the ever-popular cowboy and Indians classics.

Campbell's Steel Town Theaters

Neighborhood theaters became a significant part of life in the industrial suburb of Campbell, Ohio. The city of Campbell was originally known as the village of East Youngstown, a name adopted from a plat of land situated north of Oak Street on Youngstown's east side and west of Lansdowne. Until the 1900s, much of the area remained farmland, owned by the Blackburns, Robinsons, Creeds and other prominent families. In 1900, area investors incorporated the Youngstown Iron Sheet and Tube Company in neighboring Youngstown. After much scouting, the new company purchased undeveloped land in East Youngstown for what became known as the Campbell Works, leading to the incorporation of the village of East Youngstown. Jobs in iron and steel acted like a magnet for young European immigrants, many of them single men, looking for new opportunities.

What these immigrants found was a booming town thoroughly unprepared to properly house newcomers. The population grew 126 percent between 1910 and 1920, but the village's infrastructure did not keep pace. Workers and families usually lived in depressing dives along often-unpaved streets. In some places, as many as twenty boarders stayed in a single windowless basement. Out of this bleak landscape came the first primitive theaters.

East Youngstown (later Campbell) never developed a geographical downtown, but the area around Robinson Road and Wilson Avenue became a commercial corridor. Two early theaters developed in this corridor. "We had two theaters: the 'new show' and the 'old show,'" Charles Testa recounted. "The old show was on Short Street and Robinson Road....The new show was up on...where the post office is at Robinson Road."[54] The "old show" belonged to James Hodgekins and was known as the Hodgekins Home Theater. Thomas Birmingham owned the "new show," located at 3408 Wilson Avenue. Interestingly enough, East Youngstown almost hosted a third theater in 1916. John Lisko, bowling alley and saloon owner, announced plans to open a moving picture theater at 34 Robinson Road in late 1914. Lisko envisioned seating for as many as three hundred in the new theater until one of the most violent labor strikes in American history interrupted his plans.

In early 1916, striking workers at Youngstown Sheet and Tube and Republic Iron and Steel confronted police and company guards in what became a violent shoot-out. A riot quickly erupted in the heart of the community. "Practically the entire business section of East Youngstown has been wiped from the map," the *Youngstown Vindicator* reported in the conflagration's aftermath.[55] Lisko's property, and with it his dreams of a new theater, burned to the ground, and he left East Youngstown soon afterward. Birmingham's theater and the Home Theater sustained heavy damage but survived the rioting. The riot itself, while devastating, provided the impetus for the gradual improvement of the area's infrastructure, which included the building of safe and affordable housing.

Apart from dancing, almost no modern entertainment options existed in the area during the 1920s and 1930s. "Very few people had radios," Bill Kish remembered. "We had a neighbor next door who had one of what they called a crystal radio." But for too many, the lure of bars and gambling proved too tempting. More than a few wives found themselves at taverns or gambling dens on payday, trying to coax their wayward husbands home. The local movie theaters during this time, while often dirty and dangerous, provided one of the few outlets for mass entertainment outside of vice.

Several theaters served the community during the Roaring Twenties and the Great Depression. The Hodgekins Home Theater survived during the early Depression years, as did the Victoria Theater on Robinson Road. According to the memories of Bill Kish, Campbell's early theaters were a rather crude experience. "The first show I went to was back when I was younger," he said. "They had a Victrola playing a record, and then they had *Tarzan* showing, the picture jumping up [and down]....A guy walked up and down the aisle selling pop, so what these kids would do, they wouldn't want to go to the bathroom—they'd go in the pop bottle and roll it down [the aisle]."[56]

The Hodgekins Home Theater was one of Campbell's earliest moving picture houses. *Courtesy of Mike Parise.*

The antics of children at the local theater probably seemed minor compared to the area's formidable notoriety during the 1930s. East Youngstown, which became a city in 1922, could never quite shake the infamy brought by the 1916 riot, so in 1926 the city was renamed Campbell, after James Campbell, president of the Youngstown Sheet and Tube Company. Still, the reputation persisted. Upon conducting a multi-year study on gangs in the early 1930s, David W. Maurer, a professor at Ohio State University, dubbed Campbell "the toughest place in the U.S."[57]

After the Home Theater closed, the Palace Theater opened in the same location around 1934. Located off Short Street—steel workers commonly gathered near there anytime there was a strike—the Palace provided an afternoon's escape from the realities of the Depression outside. "We'd hang around my dad Sunday morning…until he gave us a nickel to go to the show," Henry Testa explained. "He knew what we wanted, but he'd tease us, you know, and make like he wasn't going to give us anything. Then we'd go down to the show, and we'd stay and see it maybe two or three times. That was our whole day Sunday."[58]

The Testa children were not alone in spending long afternoons at the theater. "My brother and I went to see *The Mummy* down at the Palace," William Peyko remembered. "Because of the dark we got separated, but it wasn't a very big place. But not long after the beginning of the movie, I ended up on my brother's lap."

The Palace employed more sophisticated and frequent advertising, but it was a tough theater for a tough town. Local merchants—including Bernard Lumber, the O.K. Pool Room and the Campbell Electric Shop—occasionally gave free promotional tickets to the Palace to any customer buying more than fifty cents worth of merchandise. Yet for all its patronage, the theater became known as a firetrap. In 1938, several firemen nearly perished after a blaze ignited in the projection room. Theatergoers could see the flames behind the screen as the inferno started, yet they filed out calmly and without incident. It was the third fire in eight years, but the people of Campbell, ever the hardened souls, took it in stride.

The theater's later years were buoyed by the job stability and prosperity brought by World War II, if only temporarily. Men headed overseas, and many women manned the steel jobs of wartime industry. Campbell became one of the most economically successful small cities in the nation, attracting the attention of Peter Wellman, Mahoning Valley's most successful theater owner.[59] Wellman already controlled the Palace Theater in Hubbard when

A notorious firetrap, the Palace Theater replaced the Home Theater in the early 1930s. *Courtesy of Struthers Historical Society.*

he obtained the Campbell Palace. However, toward the end of the war, the Palace in Campbell permanently closed.

In 1942, the Bell Theater opened at the corner of Washington Street and Robinson Road. A charming neighborhood theater on a hill, it became an important part of an extended business district. "Down at the bottom of Robinson Road was the area of all the stores," Helen Tarcy recalled. "There was a barbershop down there and a clothing store. Kroger's was down there at one time; across the street was an Isaly's store where you could get lunches and your ice cream cones."[60]

The Bell rapidly transformed into a neighborhood institution. "I went to the Bell after the war," William Peyko recollected. "It had been built brand new and was modern and up to date." The Bell could accommodate around two hundred people with rows of eight seats on the far sides and fifteen in the center aisles. Early admission prices were typically ten cents for children and twenty-five cents for adults.

Denny Brayer attended the Bell regularly as a young boy in the 1950s. "All the kids in the neighborhood would walk down to the theater on Saturdays in the winter," he noted. "It opened at one, and they always had kids' movies: a cowboy movie and usually a comedy or something. It was always a double feature, newsreels and sometimes a fifteen-minute serial that they would show on consecutive Saturdays. It only cost us a quarter to get in."

In 1957, the Bell opened under the management of Carl Petrella, a World War II veteran and projectionist. Petrella's tenure at the theater was very much a family affair—a dramatic departure from today's homogenized corporate chains. He often gave neighborhood children who could not afford the admission chores to do around the theater as a kind of barter. Campbell still had its tough side: gambling continued to be a mainstay in the city, and local gangster and future Mahoning Valley Mafia boss Lenine "Lenny" Strollo lived almost next door to the theater. However, the Bell represented the hardworking, family side of a town that citizens dubbed the "City of Churches." Petrella's son, Mike, explained how the Bell fit into a community-oriented city during a much simpler time:

A lot of the people around there worked down in the mills. They weren't wealthy people, and they always had big families. But there was a kind of bond between the people. You'd look out for each other's kids. There were families that would drop off their kids at the Bell, and they knew my mother would keep an eye on them while they were out shopping. It was a different time and a different place, a trusting time where you could leave your children at a place like that.

But change the times did, and the Bell closed in 1961. After almost fifty years, the city's theater tradition had ended. Television came to dominate family entertainment, and gradually the neighborhood theater became a thing of the past.

The Struthers Theater Legacy

In nearby Struthers, Ohio, the first neighborhood theater opened at a relatively early date. The A-Mus-U Theater began operating in the fall of 1912 at 158 South Bridge Street. It was owned by Patrick Kelley, who also ran Kelley Park in Leetonia, Ohio, and John Tigue, owner of Struthers's first bowling alley. The new moving picture house, with a capacity of three hundred, played three standing room–only shows opening night. Local musicians provided the orchestral accompaniment; an automatic orchestra later replaced them. Numerous "auto parties" of Youngstown motorists drove in to see the premiere of Mahoning Valley's newest theater.

Future Birmingham, Alabama theater manager Harry Curl began his career in the business working for the A-Mus-U. "My first job was handing out handbills for the theater," he recalled. "They changed the features daily, and the handbills had the weekly schedule. I'd give them to people, put them in front doors."[61] Curl absorbed the inner workings of the business, eventually becoming an usher at the theater before moving south to continue in the business. Yet just like many other children in Struthers at the time, he grew up in the A-Mus-U watching the likes of Douglas Fairbanks, Pearl White and Tom Mix on the big screen.

In 1920, the village of Struthers became a city. The new city's population increased a mindboggling 92 percent during the Roaring Twenties; new homes, usually situated on lots measuring forty-five by one hundred feet, quickly sprang up.[62] In the 1930s, after more than twenty years as the area's sole theater, the A-Mus-U was joined by a new theater more becoming to a growing city.

As the country continued to emerge from the Great Depression, the Ritz Theater opened to a jubilant city in 1937. The Ritz was the brainchild of theater entrepreneur Clarence J. Vogel, a Wellsville, Ohio resident with a long background in the business; the Ritz became a part of his association of eight theaters in the tri-state area. Situated on Bridge Street in downtown Struthers, it served 470 patrons in air-conditioned comfort. "We feel that the town will appreciate a good show," manager George Imbrie commented. "Other theaters in the association have always taken care of the public wants, and we want to fit our plans and service to the desires of Struthers."[63]

The Ritz sported a blue-and-gold marquee that welcomed customers into a cream-colored lobby with gold brocade paneling over the interior walls. Seats in the auditorium were festooned with red-and-orange metal shields on the sides. "It's the Ritz for the best in pictures," was the theater's motto. The Ritz also touted its use of a Picture-Fone sound system, something lacking at the A-Mus-U. Unfortunately, the theater's success proved to be short-lived for Vogel, who died in a tragic accident in 1939 while building another movie house.

The city fathers bragged that the Ritz was the symbolic cap on a large building boom. "Struthers has always been more substantial and a better town from the standpoint of business and living conditions than other cities in this region," Mayor T.A. Roberts explained. Prior to the Ritz, the northern section of Bridge Street languished in the shadow of the Struthers Iron and Steel Company. Nearby, the Reynolds business block was built on Bridge Street, along with a creamery, a dress shop, a beauty shop, a dry cleaners and more small businesses. A branch of the Youngstown Public Library followed. A new post office was also in the making, along with a

The Ritz Theater's marquee lights up Bridge Street in downtown Struthers, circa 1938. *Courtesy of Struthers Historical Society.*

stadium—part of the many Works Progress Administration projects going on in the area. The New Deal Restaurant, one of several businesses in Mahoning Valley named for Roosevelt's popular program, was the Ritz's neighbor. After attending the theater, patrons could walk to the New Deal or to Rip's Café for a meal and dancing.

The Ritz operated in a city where the steel industry was omnipresent. Musician Mike Roncone, born in Struthers and briefly a laborer in the local mills, recalled the environmental impact of the mills: "You'd come out of the mill after a shift and you could look up and see the graphite blowing around in the sunlight....Everything

Bill O'Hara and Lillian Heckel pose in the doorway of the Ritz Theater in 1945. *Courtesy of Patricia Ringos Beach.*

was very dirty." As a child, Roncone, like countless other children, went to the Ritz Theater or the Valley Theater (formerly known as the A-Mus-U) for an escape. "Believe it or not, Struthers had two theaters at the same time," he explained. "I used to go to the show every Sunday to see things like Abbott and Costello, though they didn't often have the cowboy movies I liked; I'd have to go to downtown Youngstown to see those."

Al Tombo, who later worked at the Ritz with his brother, remembered children working at any odd job they could find in order to afford a show at the theater. "We used to always work," he said. "I'll tell you. When I was a kid, we used to work in bowling alleys. I used to want to go to the show. Like I said, all of us kids from Struthers used to sell bottles or anything. We'd find something to do: clean windows downtown and go to the movie down at the Ritz."[64]

"The Ritz in downtown Struthers was our source of real entertainment," Gary Hoxworth explained. "For ten cents each we could go see John Wayne, Bob Hope, Bing Crosby, Martin and Lewis and Francis the Talking Mule....I got used to paying ten or fifteen cents to see a movie, so I was really shocked by the price when we went to see *The Ten Commandments* at the Palace Theater in Youngstown. It cost ninety cents to get in for the show! You could have knocked me over with a bulldozer!"

A trip to the Ritz provided a real treat for the many children who grew up in economically trying circumstances. "I lived in Dog Patch," George Hall explained. "It was up on the hill in Struthers. There would be four or five empty lots, a shack house, another few empty lots and then another old place. That's why they called it Dog Patch. My mother didn't allow me to go to the theater; she was very religious. So I'd sneak down to the Ritz with a buddy of mine. We'd get ten cents together somehow and go down to the movies for the day."

The 1950s turned out to be the last hurrah for the Ritz. During the decade, the theater featured such hits as *The Big Sky*, with Kirk Douglas; *City Beneath the Sea*, with Anthony Quinn; and *Montana Belle*, with Jane Russell. Faced with the rise of television and the popularity of drive-in theaters, smaller neighborhood movie houses found it difficult to survive. By 1960, even downtown Youngstown theaters were having difficulties. Declining attendance led to the shuttering of the Ritz in late 1960, closing the last chapter in Struthers's theatrical history.

The Roxy Comes to Canfield

Far beyond the smoke and soot of Campbell and Struthers, Canfield, Ohio—predominately a rural area—received its own neighborhood theater just as World War II began in Europe. Until the mid-1870s, Canfield, located at the geographic heart of Mahoning County, served as the county seat. That honor passed to the rapidly growing city of Youngstown in 1876. Loss of the county seat hurt Canfield, which from then on became primarily known for hosting the ever-popular Canfield Fair.

By 1930, only 1,015 people inhabited the village. Most of the business district centered on the village green, bordered by Broad Street and what is now U.S. Route 224. A ballroom above a local hardware store provided one of the few entertainment outlets; the local Isaly's and a soda fountain were some of the only businesses where young people could gather. That all changed in 1936.

During the summer of 1935, the first Works Progress Administration projects began in Mahoning County. By early 1936, eight thousand men and women were working for the WPA.[65] All manner of projects occupied them, from school construction to paving jobs—$65,000 was allotted for a Canfield community center, and area organizations and individuals donated

The WPA Memorial Building in Canfield became home to the Roxy Theater in 1939.
Courtesy of the author.

another $60,000. Aaron Wiesner, a local entrepreneur, gifted the land for the new building on South Broad Street near the village green.

Initial plans for the building, ultimately rejected by the WPA, called for using imported stone. Instead, the builders used sandstone from Dean Hill Quarry in Canfield. Architects W.H. Cook and W. Canfield of Youngstown designed a Colonial Revival look for the structure. A committee composed of several community organizations and representatives of the village decided that the new project should be a multipurpose space with diverse facilities.

In 1936, the community laid the cornerstone for the WPA Memorial Building. Officials sealed several items into the cornerstone: pictures of the mayor, Aaron Wiesner; the rosters of the local Argus Masonic Lodge, the Boy Scouts and the American Legion; copies of the *Mahoning Dispatch*, the *Youngstown Vindicator* and the *Youngstown Telegram*; and photographs of U.S. Senator Robert Bulkley and President Franklin Roosevelt. "This is a notable day for Canfield," Mayor Robert Manchester proclaimed at the time. "Make this building your home. It's your home."[66]

The new community building featured a bowling alley in the basement and a large space for the American Legion on the second floor, along with a ballroom and a new branch of the Reuben McMillan Free Library. A stage measuring forty-five by twenty feet (with attached dressing rooms) and an auditorium capable of seating 250 were located on the first floor. This became the genesis of the Roxy Theater.

Initially, the Village Theater, a local drama club, used the stage for community plays. The Canfield Community Theater Group also used the auditorium to show films twice a week. Motion pictures had been shown at various times in Canfield since at least 1917, when the Movie Club of Canfield screened various five-reel pictures at the town hall. The Canfield Community Theater Group, however, soon morphed into a commercial theater, Canfield's first.

The Roxy Theater opened on the first floor in late summer of 1939. *Our Leading Citizen*, with Susan Hayward, and *Susannah of the Mountains*, with Shirley Temple, were the opening night's films. Admission was ten cents for children and twenty cents for adults. Frank Cavanaugh attended the Roxy regularly as a youth, and his father acted on the stage in local theater productions. "As you walked in the doors that face the streets, you went up a couple of stairs and the theater was straight ahead," he remembered. "My uncle and aunt lived near there in a brick house. We always went there for Thanksgiving, and my sister and I were allowed to walk to the theater, which was always open on holidays. And if you went on a date, you paid your own way and met your date inside the theater."

The Roxy was a no-frills experience—no popcorn or soda was offered for sale—yet its existence symbolized how far and wide neighborhood theaters had spread. Urban theatergoers in the early 1940s faced an abundance of local movie options nearby, regardless of their location in Mahoning Valley. The Roxy represented the only theater in a Youngstown suburb, outside the Newport Theater in suburban Boardman. In Youngstown, apart from the six theaters downtown, one could attend the Foster or the Uptown on the south side; the Schenley and Mahoning, both located on the west side; the Home, Lincoln and Wilson on the east side; or the Center Theater, situated between the steel mills on Center Street. Struthers featured the Ritz and the Valley. Campbell showcased the Palace and the Bell. Peter Wellman's New Mock and Wellman Theaters dominated Girard, and Niles was home to the Warner Theater, McKinley and Butler.

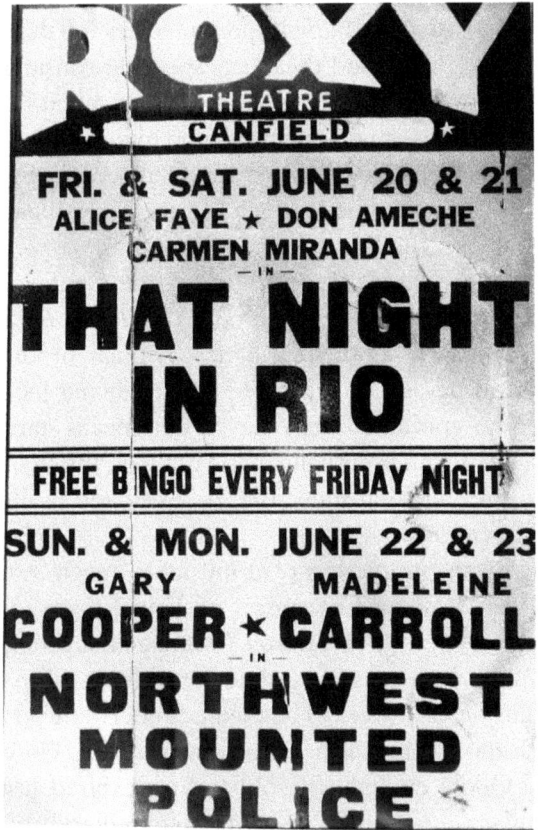

Right: An old poster from the Roxy advertises an upcoming show, circa 1941. *Courtesy of the author.*

Below: The Canfield Players, a live theatrical group, also called the Roxy Theater home. *Courtesy of Doris and Frank Cavanaugh.*

The Roxy certainly represented one of the smaller and more intimate of the neighborhood theaters, especially considering its lack of a stand-alone location. The theater always reserved a seat for Mrs. Hawkins, the wife of a local dentist, and junior high and high school kids had free rein over the back rows. The Roxy featured the Gene Autry, Roy Rogers and Frank Sinatra films at its matinees, much like the other theaters. On certain nights, bingo took over the Roxy.

The Roxy's stage also hosted the Canfield Players, descendants of the Village Theater acting group. *Our Town*, *The Man Who Came to Dinner* and *Harvey* were among their most popular productions. The Canfield Players might be best remembered for producing Joe Flynn. Born in Youngstown, Flynn graduated from Rayen but got his start directing plays on the Roxy stage. Flynn eventually made it big on the small and large screens—starring in the television show *McHale's Navy* and in films such as *Son of Flubber* and *The Love Bug*.

By the beginning of 1950, after much struggling, the Roxy closed. In 1951, Rawson Enterprises of Youngstown took over the old Roxy space, renaming it "Our Theater." Management completely redecorated the entire auditorium space, including the addition of an updated screen; films showed four nights a week. The theater underwent yet another name change, to the Grand Theater, in 1952 before eventually closing completely.

Oddly enough, the old theater expired just as Canfield—situated at a higher elevation far from the steel mills—began to attract residents fleeing neighboring Youngstown for suburban life. The old Roxy passed into memory only years before Canfield became known as one of the "cleanest" communities in the country and one of the "best communities" in America with a population under twenty-five thousand. Unlike many other local theater buildings, the WPA Memorial Building survived and today is mostly home to commercial office space and a deli. Only the old Roxy Theater signs in the basement reveal that a theater once occupied the premises.

GIRARD AND HUBBARD

Welcome to Wellman's Theater Town

For a small city, Girard, Ohio, is steeped in theater history: from the Luna to the Wellman, a series of movie houses served the area for nearly sixty years.

Girard was principally associated with Peter Wellman, Mahoning Valley's leading theater entrepreneur. His theaters, the New Mock and the Wellman, gave this small community a long-standing and successful theater scene. And long after they vanished, the legacy of Wellman and his cinemas remain etched in the area's history.

In 1900, about 2,500 people lived in the village of Girard. Much like its neighbor, Youngstown, Girard's economy revolved around iron and the growing steel industry. The Ohio Leather Works had just opened and went on to become the largest calf leather processing plant in the country. The Youngstown Sheet and Tube Brier Hill Works provided a readily available source of jobs for a growing community.

Most local amusements centered on basic live entertainment. The area's big draw was an amusement park, Squaw Creek Park, later changed to Avon Park. Mule races, baseball games, the Ferris wheel, a zoo and other attractions drew capacity crowds to Avon on a regular basis. It was not until about 1910 that the first moving picture shows appeared in Girard.

The film journal *Motography* reported in 1911 that Girard's Luna Theater had been fully remodeled "as one of the most modern and up-to-date moving picture theaters in the country, under the management of Percy L. Pennock."[67] The Luna originally faced the Bijou Theater, of which little is known, on West Liberty Street. E.R. Mateer vividly recalled the Luna during its early years. "When we had newspaper concessions we could put their handbills in the papers, and for this we had passes for both theaters and could go in and out at will," he said. "I remember I often took tickets, rewound reels and other odd jobs. Between reels there was either a piano interlude or a solo."[68]

In 1915, the Mock Theater opened in the heart of West Liberty Street. The Mock's owner, Jacob "Jake" Mock, was well known in the Mahoning Valley amusement world. He ran one of the most profitable concessions at Avon Park and first introduced doll lamps to the area, which became a fad. Spotting trends became Mock's stock in trade, and the theater business was just one more growing industry for him to pursue. Several years after he opened the theater, Mock pioneered Girard's first miniature golf course, a widely popular trend at the time. Yet his theater achieved its real fame under the ownership of another entrepreneur—a man with a real vision for local theaters.

Peter Wellman came from very humble beginnings. As a young boy, he made the trip from his native Greece to Ellis Island alone. The immigration authorities were clueless as to how to pronounce his name, so they asked for the meaning of his surname, which roughly translated to "the man who

Theater owner Peter Wellman (*right*) and an unknown individual pose with Robby the Robot. *Courtesy of Girard Historical Society.*

brings water from the well." They quickly named him Wellman. He took his first job at a theater but later bought two lunchrooms. Wellman owned his first picture house by age twenty-three; several years later, he acquired the Strand Theater in Farrell, Pennsylvania.

He purchased the Mock Theater in Girard in 1934 and changed its name to Wellman (he originally planned on calling it the Liberty). Sometime around 1937, he built another theater almost next door, which he dubbed the New Mock, in honor of Jacob Mock, who died in 1936. The Wellman could seat five hundred and the New Mock about seven hundred. Wellman voiced his confidence that the new business block would set an example for the city. "If Girard is to grow and prosper and develop as a good business and industrial center in its own right, it will have to compete with the bigger cities in the appearance of its own business section," he declared. "If we can have a modern, up-to-date business section in this town, we don't need to worry about how to keep our local businesses at home."[69]

Aside from other numerous real estate holdings, he also owned the Mahoning Country Club, which began hosting a yearly PGA tournament with such notables as Craig Wood, Ben Hogan and Gene Sarazen. Bing Crosby became fast friends with Wellman, playing golf with him at the country club whenever he was in town to see his wife perform with the Kenley Players in Warren.

During the 1940s, Wellman operated fourteen different local theaters, including the Uptown (with Stephen Foster), the Victory, the Hubbard and Campbell Palace, the Mahoning, Schenley, Home, Wellman, New Mock, Belmont and Newport, as well as the North Side, South Side and West Side Drive-Ins. He also controlled the Shane Drive-In (later called the Pymatuning Lake Drive-In) in Andover and the Howard Theater in Ashtabula. However, his home remained in Girard with his first two local theaters.

Wellman's theaters were a home away from home for many Girard youths. Jack Carlton's grandmother owned a store, My Lady Shop, on State Street downtown. Whenever he could, he made a trip to the theaters after visiting her. "They [Wellman and New Mock] showed a lot of war films," Carlton noted. "My aunt objected to us going to one particular movie, because it was awfully bloody—that type of thing. And when we were all downtown, we decided we really needed to see that movie. Of course we got found out."

Along with war films, Girard theaters were known for the wildly popular double features and the midnight "spook shows," usually with a gag thrown in. When *Frankenstein* and *The Wolf Man* played on a Saturday night, management warned, "There'll be plenty of ambulances on hand to rush those who have fainted to the nearest physician. There'll be plenty of strong-armed ushers to carry out the patrons who have grown too weak from terror to be able to walk alone." Typically, the Wellman played more family-friendly fare, and the New Mock showed more adult-style films. Together, they offered the community a breadth of viewing experiences.

The New Mock and Wellman Theaters entertained generations of Girard theatergoers. *Courtesy of Girard Historical Society.*

The New Mock and Wellman were so successful because of Wellman himself. Known for his tireless work habits, he labored from early in the morning through closing at eleven o'clock at night. He oversaw the operations of many theaters but frequently could be seen sweeping the sidewalk in front of the New Mock and Wellman on West Liberty Street. He regularly greeted customers in the lobby and worked on the advertising and marketing. But most all of, Wellman just loved the entertainment business. When he was introduced to Ohio governor James Rhodes, Wellman said, "Governor, the name is not important. I'm just the man in Girard who makes people happy."[70]

In 1959, after many years in the business, Wellman began selling off the last of his theaters, including those in Girard. Albert Garfield, a former theater manager involved in the vending business, took over both theaters. "I've always wanted to own my own theaters," he said at the time. "Girard seems to be a progressive town, and I'm proud to be here."[71] Garfield leased the New Mock to Stephen Foster, owner of Youngstown's Uptown Theater, and changed the name of the Wellman to the Art Guild in 1961. The Art Guild primarily played art house–style films and adult fare, including films such as *Pepe*, *Exodus* and *La Dolce Vita*.

By the early 1960s, Mahoning Valley theaters located outside suburban areas were struggling. Many neighborhood theaters folded in the late 1950s or early 1960s; the Art Guild proved no exception. The theater struggled to find an audience, and Garfield transformed it into the Girard Roller Palace, an indoor roller-skating rink. His daughter, Sharon Williams Garfield, remembered some of the other wilder uses for the old theater. "He even rigged up netting inside the Wellman to periodically turn it into a [golf] driving range for him and his buddies," she explained.

After giving up his theaters and going into semi-retirement, Wellman reconsidered. He bought back the Newport Theater, and in 1963 he reacquired the New Mock from Stephen Foster, which he renamed the Wellman Theater. The Girard Roller Palace survived only a few years and closed, becoming Bill's Furniture and Appliance. By 1966, Wellman was focused on opening the Wedgewood Cinema in Austintown. Despite his other commitments, he regularly ventured to Girard. "I love this town," Wellman told a friend in 1969. "I don't have to come here anymore. I'm busy at the Wedgewood, and I'm not getting any younger. But this town

Girard's Wellman Theater, circa 1954. *Courtesy of Girard Historical Society.*

has been good to me. The people have been good to me. Girard gave Peter Wellman his start. And I love to come here to see my old friends."[72] Days later, he died at the age of sixty-seven.

The Wellman, under the management of George Pappas and his wife, began to show edgier fare—such as Russ Meyer's *Vixen*—before transforming into an adult theater, Cinema I, in 1969. By this time, the Wellman Theater had outlived all the neighborhood theaters in Campbell, Struthers, Niles and most of those in Youngstown. A public backlash quickly ensued against Cinema I. Janet Kennedy, a waitress at nearby Diamond's Restaurant, said, "What I want to know is what the kids in Girard are going to do now?" Girard resident Sally Arnott looked at the situation from another angle. "Girard didn't support its only theater, and as a result, the couple [the Pappases] have to show what people seem to want the most!"[73]

Cinema I tried to placate the city by reverting to showing non-adult films, only to see attendance drop mightily by mid-1970. "We need at least fifty to break even each night," George Pappas explained in July 1970. "But when only two or three people show up, we give them back their money, close up and go home."[74] The theater eventually switched back to showing adult films, and Cinema I remained open for another decade.

In 2002, Reverend Robert E. Saylor converted the old Wellman Theater into Faith Center of World Ministries. Church music replaced the sounds of motion pictures, and a cross went up where the old screen once stood. Girard's theater culture had long since passed, but Reverend Saylor still entertained the idea of showing films someday in the old place. Somewhere, Peter Wellman, the devout Christian, might have been smiling. Faith Center of World Ministries no longer occupies the building today, but the old Wellman/New Mock building remains one of Mahoning Valley's last theater buildings left standing.

Hubbard's Palace

A small theater tucked into a corner on West Liberty Street in Hubbard, Ohio, incredibly became a community icon for nearly a half century. The Palace Theater entertained generations of Hubbard's children, providing an afternoon getaway into a world of westerns, science fiction monsters and things that go bump in the night. A family-owned establishment, the Palace was a far cry from today's corporate-owned cinemas. For those who passed through its modest doors, the Palace remains indelibly etched in

Hubbard's Palace Theater remained open longer than most neighborhood theaters in the Mahoning Valley. *Courtesy of Barbara Emch.*

their minds along with the goodness of childhood and the memories of many a pleasant weekend afternoon.

In the early 1920s, slightly over three thousand people lived in the small Trumbull County Township. Life in Hubbard revolved around simple pleasures and modest entertainments. Inspired by the story of Youngstown's Warner brothers, a local businessman known as "Pappy" Wolf began to investigate the possibility of opening a theater in Hubbard. The owner of a local clothing store, Wolf opened the Liberty Theater to the public during the economic expansion of the Roaring Twenties.

The Liberty quickly began to participate in something called "Paramount Week" during the mid-1920s. During that week, exhibitors involved with the program showed nothing but Paramount Pictures. This practice was essentially a prelude to "block booking," which began in the early 1930s, when independent theater owners were essentially forced to exhibit package deals from studios in order to get access to films with top stars.[75] The Liberty in Hubbard and the Liberty in East Palestine both participated in Paramount Week.

Silent films predominated during the early years; piano music provided the accompaniment. Warner Vitaphone sound on disk appeared in the late 1920s. Eventually, the RCA Photophone system for syncing sound arrived at the Liberty sometime in the early 1930s. After Donald Hegfield began running the theater in the 1930s, some of the old equipment still remained. "When we came up there, up in the [projection] booth, there was still a table up there where they used to play records," Hegfield remembered. "The talking was on the record, see, and it had to be synchronized with the film."[76]

Hegfield moved to Hubbard in 1934 from Ashtabula, Ohio. A recent high school graduate, he found a job managing the Liberty. Born in 1914, Hegfield spent his working life in the theater business. His uncle ran the Palace Theater in Campbell and the Capitol Theater in Farrell, Pennsylvania; his aunt managed an Ashtabula theater at one point. The Palace reached its height of popularity while Hegfield was at the helm.

After an initial remodel in 1934, the theater received another upgrade in 1938. By that time, it was known as the Palace. The theater had no restrooms prior to 1938; patrons used the facilities at a nearby gas station. Originally, the Liberty could seat between 175 and 190 patrons. The new and improved Palace could seat a little more than 300 after the building was expanded.

It was rare for a theater to invest so much in improvements during the Great Depression, at a time when some of the large movie palaces in downtown Youngstown teetered on the edge of closing. "In that Depression there were plenty of people out of work," Hegfield later recollected. "By the time we got down here in 1934, everything started picking up. The theater always did pretty good business. We had them standing in line there outside. Of course, the theater was smaller....Still, there would be lines going around the corner, waiting to get into the second show."[77]

During the 1940s, the Palace came into the hands of Peter Wellman. One of Wellman's main innovations was to bring Bank Night to Hubbard. The origins of Bank Night, which started in Colorado but quickly spread, date back to the beginning of the Depression. Theaters, desperate to attract audiences, adopted Bank Night, along with something called "Dish Night," as a means to bring crowds back in big numbers.

Bank Night worked like a lottery: patrons signed their names to a register, which contained a number next to it. That number was then put into the drawing. Customers need not buy a ticket to enter the drawing, although many did. Winners received a cash prize. According to historian Kathryn H. Fuller-Seeley, "Small towns across America came to a standstill on Bank Night because everyone was in the theater or was standing outside the packed house, straining to hear the winner announced over a loudspeaker attached to the marquee. It did not matter what picture was showing at the theater on Bank Night because people came for the drawing, not the film."[78]

Hubbard's Palace Theater, circa 1956. *Courtesy of Emanuel Mageros.*

Wellman also held Dish Nights. Much like movie theaters, manufacturers of dinner ware suffered during the Depression. The Salem China Company, Homer Laughlin and others often partnered with theaters, offering a different piece of complimentary tableware every week for movie patrons. Dish Night was an enormous hit with housewives, although it never matched the popularity of Bank Night. Later, giveaways involving toys were held for kiddie matinees.

Promotions like Dish and Bank Night kept adults going to the Palace. However, by the 1950s, the theater was predominately frequented by children and teenagers. The pull of television kept adults at home, but children of the baby boom in Hubbard came to know the Palace as a weekend home away from home. Mary Ann Lark spent many happy afternoons at Palace Theater during her youth. "We went every Sunday," she explained. "My mom would give us a quarter—we had fifteen cents for popcorn or candy, and the rest was for admission. When we were going, all they usually showed were cowboy movies and the like. When I was very little, they had an air force base out at Brookfield. The theater would be packed with men in brown uniforms; they were in there all the time."

Emanuel Mageros worked at the Palace as an usher. "When you walked in the door, inside the lobby was a big mirror with tiles all around it," he mentioned. "You then went past the candy and popcorn counter....There was even a little mezzanine on the third floor. On Saturdays they held a drawing. You got a popcorn box, put your name on the lid and tore it off for the drawing. If you won, you got a free ticket to a show."

Teens had their run of the theater too. "All of the lovers would sit off in the corners," Mageros remembered. According to Mary Ann Lark, "Parents didn't allow you to have a boyfriend or a girlfriend until you were 16 years old, so the Palace Theater was a great place to meet and 'neck.' It was really dark in there, but everyone knew what everyone else was doing. We would never tell. What went on in the Palace Theater stayed in the Palace Theater!"[79]

The theater passed through a variety of hands but continued to have financial difficulties, and in 1958, it closed. "It is unfortunate that this had to happen," owner Steve Vernarsky commented at the time. "But there is nothing else that can be done at this time." In 1959, Donald Hegfield bought the theater and reopened it. It survived the entire decade of the 1960s while most of its counterparts in surrounding communities shuttered during the time of John F. Kennedy's presidency.

Hegfield was ready to back away from running the day-to-day operations of the Palace by the early 1970s, and he rented the theater to Roger Jones. But

Hegfield continued to run the projector. An employee of Packard Electric, Jones had long dreamed of owning of a theater. "Dad loved movies," son Bryan Jones recalled. "He grew up going to theaters in downtown Sharon, where they'd have cartoons and serials, and you could watch movies all day."

Unable to get first-run films from distributors, Jones turned to monster movies, science fiction and the occasional racy film to bring people into the theater: *Godzilla vs. The Smog Monster*, *Frogs*, *The Biscuit Eater*, *Encounter with the Unknown* and other such fare appealed to the young audiences. A typical showing featured two Three Stooges comedies, cartoons and a film like *Godzilla's Revenge*, all for seventy-five cents. "Godzilla movies were my dad's biggest hits," Jones recalled. "I remember specifically when *Destroy All Monsters* played. Every seat was full, and people were sitting on the floor." A series of adult-oriented films from Europe became popular stateside during the late 1960s and early 1970s. Jones screened one such film, *Dagmar's Hot Pants, Inc.*, which landed him in trouble with many in the community.

Jones regularly picked up the films at the Greyhound bus station in downtown Youngstown, and every Saturday the family ventured to downtown Sharon to purchase popcorn. The Palace even had an old cash register from the former Gable Theater in Sharon. Not far from the cash register were the cotton candy machine, snow cones and the Jetspray dispenser. These details, not often found in small theaters, were all part of Jones's personal touch.

Tylee Park now stands on the site of the former Palace. *Photo by the author.*

The Palace continued to show popular films such as *A Clockwork Orange* and *Play Misty for Me*. However, the lack of first-run films hurt the theater. By the time Jones received offers for first-run films like the *Godfather Part II*, it was too late. The Palace closed in 1974. "As I grew up and became an adult, every time I drove through Hubbard I'd look over at the Palace," Bryan Jones explained. "And I'd tell my friends about its stories....It was an important part of this town for decades."

The Joseph Baldine administration, looking to build a pedestrian mall resembling the one in downtown Youngstown, targeted the theater for demolition as early as 1972. Yet the old building lingered on for years, eventually becoming a junk shop. The former Palace still stood, abandoned, in 1988. That year, a petition to have the building torn down and the lot crafted into a park reached the Hubbard City Council. After demolition, the site was turned into Tylee Park, named after Samuel Tylee, Hubbard's first settler.

The children who plant flowers at Tylee Park every year might not know anything of the Palace; that era has long passed. Television, the Internet, video games and various smart devices have long since replaced the neighborhood theater, but for those who remember it, nothing will replace the fond memories of afternoons spent at Hubbard's beloved theater.

Part 4

WARREN AND THE ROBINS LEGACY

THE THEATERS OF WARREN

Only eighteen or so miles from Youngstown is the city of Warren, the second largest in the Mahoning Valley. Warren, along with Youngstown, constituted the backbone of local manufacturing might. At one time, more than sixty-three thousand people lived inside the city limits, and a variety of theaters served the hardworking people of Warren—the Robins, Daniel, Ohio and many others lined the streets of the booming downtown. For much of the twentieth century, a vibrant theater culture made Warren second only to Youngstown in terms of motion picture offerings.

The first real venue for live theater and music opened to the public in 1886 on High Street. The Warren Opera House quickly joined its Youngstown counterpart as one of the pillars of entertainment in the Mahoning Valley. Made mostly of brick and Ohio sandstone, the building also displayed touches of terra cotta, often called a construction "wonder material" in the late nineteenth century. A tower with a Far Eastern feel graced the top of the three-story building, and the second floor housed mostly private offices.

The opera house's stage measured sixty feet wide and thirty-five feet deep; it could handle all requirements for most performances and scene changes. The performers' dressing rooms were located adjacent to and beneath the stage. Gaslights for the house, which produced large volumes of heat, could be controlled from underneath the stage. A large sun burner connected by a chimney to the outside helped to simultaneously throw a large amount of light while also acting as a ventilator. The house contained eight hundred seats, which included box seats. Within a short period of time, Warren's opera house had emerged as a popular stop on the vaudeville circuit. After the opera house closed, it became the Harris-Warren Theater.

As the moving picture craze spread throughout the area in the early twentieth century, the first nickelodeons opened in Warren. Initially, a local businessman, R.W. Elliott, screened the very first crude films in the area. By 1907, the opera house began showing moving picture films before live vaudeville performances, something management referred to as "a stunt."[80] The Electric Theater, possibly the first moving picture house to operate in Warren, opened weeks later on Park Avenue. The Electric survived for a brief time, shuttering in the late summer.

A series of nickelodeons soon sprouted, one on the heels of the other. The Edisonia Theater opened at 105 Main Street the same year as the Electric Theater. It was first owned by Kibler and E.C. Porter, the latter of whom also bought Youngstown's Dreamland Theater, which briefly proved to be extraordinarily popular. And later it passed into the hands of businessman H.H. Andrews. The Theatorium opened before the Edisonia at 112 Main

The Warren Opera House, opened in 1886, eventually became the Harris-Warren Theater. *Courtesy of the* Warren Tribune.

Street; it offered both picture shows and live vaudeville. Owner D.S. Fisher later opened the Grand Theater on Main Street, which offered live music from professional musicians and an expanded stage for vaudeville productions.

In the fall of 1907, Warren's most sophisticated nickelodeon, the Dreamland Theater, opened at 7 North Park Avenue. It initially sported a piano (later replaced by a Wurlitzer Automatic Orchestra). The theater's screen measured eleven by fourteen feet, and a "board of censors" scrutinized films before they could be shown. Unlike its predecessors, it thrived for years.[81] One year after the Dreamland opened, the Crescent

Theater followed on Main Street; like the Dreamland, the Crescent survived the competition and stayed in business until 1918. In those years, downtown Warren's business district had the second-largest number of nickelodeons in the Mahoning Valley.

Warren's first proper modern theater opened on East Market Street in late 1914. The Duchess Theater, well ventilated and spacious (unlike many nickelodeons), promised to be a motion picture house worthy of a rapidly growing city. *Moving Picture World* referred to the Duchess as "one of the prettiest" theaters in northeast Ohio.[82] The theater's façade was done in terra cotta, a norm for many of the best downtown buildings in Warren and Youngstown at the time. A large arcade led patrons past the confectionery stand and into the auditorium, which, at that point, was the largest of any movie house between Cleveland and Pittsburgh. A photoplayer automatic orchestra lent the theater an air of the modern. All of its accompanying sound effects, including everything from automobile noises to galloping horse sounds, provided audiences with a lively night of silent films. Opening night's crowd included socialites from cities as close as Youngstown and as far as Ashtabula, Ohio. In 1919, the Robins Amusement Company began leasing the Duchess; in 1929, it renamed it the Ohio Theater.

Four years after the Duchess opened, and three years after the Youngstown Hippodrome, the Warren Hippodrome debuted for city audiences. Like the opera house, the Hippodrome stood three stories tall. An arcade, graced with shades of ivory and brown, decorated its entrance. The theater's auditorium featured spacious seating in mahogany and leather, a balcony and box seating. The J.J. Callow Company of Cleveland completed interior plaster and artwork around the boxes. Immediately drawing the attention of patrons, a large, elaborate oil painting dominated the top of the stage. Deep red-and-blue tapestries hung on the walls above velvet carpets. The Hippodrome also showcased a $10,000 Hillgreen-Lane organ similar to, but smaller than, the one in Youngstown's Liberty Theater.

Flags flew along the Hippodrome on opening night. Red, white and blue lights in the theater's interior matched the patriotic mood. Nearly one thousand guests filed in, and every lady present on opening night received a floral arrangement. Each seat in the house had its own ventilator underneath, which directly heated the customer in cold weather or blew air chilled by ice and driven by conduits during the summer months. The opening of the Hippodrome symbolized Warren's rising status as a manufacturing and entertainment mecca.

No one influenced Warren's theater culture more than the famed Robins family. The Robins brothers, along with Peter Wellman, became the most influential entrepreneurs in Trumbull County's entertainment world. The Robins Amusement Company controlled theaters in both Niles and Warren and built the Robins Theater, the finest movie palace in Warren. The brothers' legacy, like the Warner brothers, can be traced back to the early days of motion pictures in New Castle, Pennsylvania, and Youngstown.

Daniel Robins, future president of the Robins Amusement Company, began his career in the entertainment world at the same time as the Warner brothers in the city of New Castle. A scant ten months after opening the Cascade Theater in downtown New Castle, the Warner brothers sold their share in the business to Daniel, who helped open a vaudeville house on the premises. Daniel later ran the Bijou Theater in downtown Youngstown. A typical take from this modest enterprise was less than ten dollars for one showing to a packed house. However, it proved to be just the beginning for Robins.

An immigrant from Lithuania, Daniel intuitively understood the new business of motion pictures. He and his brother, Ben, came to run several theaters in Youngstown, including the Palace and the Dreamland Theaters, among others. Brother David began his career running a grocery store before entering the theater business. He married Annie Warner and, in 1911, opened the Rex Theater in Youngstown along with Harry Warner. After suffering setbacks with their business interests in New Castle, the Robins clan quickly regrouped.

Ben Robins began operating businesses in Sharon, Pennsylvania, and the brothers opened a circus at the same time called Robins Combined Shows. With an eye on the local theater business, the Robins brothers eventually formed Robins Enterprises Incorporated and the Robins Amusement Company. They took control of the Duchess Theater in 1919 and soon began planning their biggest project yet: the construction of the famed Robins Theater in Warren.

The Robinses' "dream theater" opened to universal acclaim in early 1923. Designed by C. Howard Crane, the architect of Youngstown's Liberty Theater and Detroit's Orchestra Hall, the Robins was a stunning building. The new theater represented a $500,000 investment, all told, in the 100 block of East Market Street. The building's exquisite exterior prominently featured terra cotta with a neoclassical Italian Renaissance design. A large marquee included two hundred separate lights, creating a blazing glow up and down the street. The exterior ticket booth included

The Robins Theater opened in 1923 and soon became the crown jewel of the Robins Amusement Company. *Courtesy of the* Warren Tribune.

an automatic ticket dispenser and a semi-automatic change machine. The interior lobby was done in the style of the Adams brothers, much like Youngstown's Liberty Theater. Paneled murals representing the four arts—drama, music, singing and dancing—were framed over the marble flooring. Two dramatic marble staircases led to the balcony.

Some of the original seats still grace the balcony of the Robins Theater. *Courtesy of the* Warren Tribune.

Patrons passed well-crafted columns and a beautiful balustrade, all done in Vermont marble, on their way toward the spacious auditorium. Indirect lighting in the auditorium mimicked the changing times of day. The walls contained hand-painted murals; horsehair was used in the plasterwork. The house could seat 1,500 patrons—1,100 on the floor and 400 in the balcony. The original wooden seats featured a carved letter *R* for Robins underneath the armrest. The seats were all later replaced, except for the balcony, where African American patrons were forced to sit prior to the civil rights era.

The Robinses planned for the new venue to be a live theater capable of handling road shows. An orchestra pit was built underneath the screen stage; builders estimated that it would take twenty-four hours to convert the house for stage shows. According to the *Warren Tribune*, "Workmen could begin building a stage while motion picture performances were continued in the theater proper. Then when the theater was closed at 11 P.M., a temporary intervening wall of lumber could be torn down, the connections to the front of the stage made and the stage playhouse ready for opening the following night."[83] Motion pictures were the core business; however, live shows such as *Auntie Mame*, starring Sylvia Sidney, appeared on the theater's stage in later years.

On opening night, a capacity crowd packed the Robins to take in the spectacle of Warren's new crown jewel. Mayor John D. McBride and Judge C.M. Wilkins received golden keys as symbolic tokens of appreciation from the Robins brothers to the citizens of Warren and Trumbull County. Long before showtime, two long lines extended far down Market Street—such was the anticipation. The American Legion band played "The Star-Spangled Banner" while flags, a representation of the Statue of Liberty and a color guard were positioned on stage. The Robins Orchestra followed the tableau with a rendition of the overture from Carl Maria von Weber's *Oberon*. A double feature of *The Speeder* and *Quincy Adams Sawyer* followed the festivities.

The Robins continued to be Warren's showcase theater for the next two decades but was joined by another Robins Amusement Company project in 1942. Thirty-five years after opening his first theater, Daniel Robins presided over the opening of the Daniel Theater on East Market Street. Despite the start of the war, Warren's theater scene continued to boom. Even Marlene Dietrich appeared in Warren in June 1942 to promote war bonds.

The opening of the Daniel represented the height of cinema popularity in Warren. Construction began in 1941. According to Daniel Robins, the theater was built to "keep up with the growth of the city," which had blossomed to almost forty-three thousand people by 1940.[84] The death of one of the brothers, Nate, as well as the war itself, led to the cancellation of any planned festivities for the theater's opening.

The tile and brick theater was formally dedicated to the deceased Ben Robins, the former vice-president of Robins Enterprises. A plaque in the theater's interior read, "This theater is dedicated to the memory of a pioneer who held faith in the betterment of the community life of Warren through the field of entertainment."[85] Unlike the Robins, the Daniel consisted of only one story. The theater's auditorium held seats for 1,200 patrons, each tastefully covered in bluish leather. Similar to the Newport

The Daniel Theater today is a storefront church. *Photo by the author.*

Theater, it contained murals, done in phosphorescent paint, on either side of the screen. Each glowed in the dark under black light. The screen itself measured eighteen by twenty-two feet. The Daniel also included a powder room for the ladies and a "den room" for the men. Two storefronts shared space with the theater itself.

The Daniel was the latest addition to Robins Enterprises. Aside from the Robins and the Ohio Theaters, the company controlled the Warner Theater in Niles, acquired in 1927, and the Butler and McKinley Theaters, also in Niles. Brother David Robins managed the Warner Theater until his death in 1941; Abe Warner himself flew back from the Warner Studios in California to attend the funeral. Daniel Robins died in late 1945 at the age of seventy, only three years after the opening of the Daniel. His death reflected the passing of a historic era in Warren's history. No other theaters have opened in downtown Warren since the Daniel in 1942.

The downtown's theater scene began to decline during the 1950s. Struggling to attract audiences, some occasionally screened adult-oriented films. Helga Wengler, a recent immigrant from Germany in 1955, found this out firsthand. Wengler commuted by bus to downtown Warren to get to her job at Packard Electric. Due to the bus schedule, she often found herself with spare time before the afternoon shift began. One day, she decided to catch a movie at the Ohio Theater.

"I was confused because I couldn't yet read English, and the banner didn't have any posters or photos of the movie," Wengler recalled. "I went in there and it was so dark. There were no lights on before the movie started. All of the sudden the movie started, and it really started to get raunchy. A guy near me started to breathe heavily. I got down on my knees and tried to sneak out of there; it was so embarrassing."

During its last year in business, the Ohio screened films such as *Teaserama* with the famous pin-up model Bettie Page. The Daniel even screened some of the early women-in-prison films from the 1950s, always billed as "adults only." Tame by today's standards, these movies often roused the ire of local censors. Yet despite this, the Ohio Theater closed in 1956. In 1958, more than seventy years after it originally opened as the Warren Opera House, the Harris-Warren Theater closed. The *Warren Tribune* accurately diagnosed the reason for its demise: "Movie houses all over the country have been having a hard time for the last decade. The beginning of the decline probably can be dated from the advent of television. Patrons who regularly attended the movies stuck to their living room easy chairs and watched this new novel media of communication bring entertainment to their homes."[86]

After more than a quarter century of being in business, the Harris-Warren closed in 1958. *Courtesy of Thomas Molocea.*

The Robins Theater continued to serve the community through good times and bad. During the 1920s, the Robins also hosted community events, including live cooking demonstrations on weekday mornings for packed houses. In 1927, the Robins became the first theater in Warren to feature Vitaphone sound. Audiences on opening night, which featured the film *Don Juan*, enjoyed the New York Philharmonic, which played before the film began. In 1933, management installed a curved, panoramic screen. At nineteen feet high and thirty feet wide, it was the largest in the city.

Mary Ann Flaviano recalled that going to the Robins was always a treat, one part of a vibrant downtown experience. "My mother didn't drive, so we would walk downtown, pay the bills and catch a matinee," she remembered. At night, the Robins often featured some of the finest live entertainment in the Mahoning Valley. "I remember going to see Louis Prima, Vaughn Monroe, a lot of those famous acts, and all of the people from the Robins would go to the Hollyhock, which was a racketeer joint nearby."

In 1974, with businesses closing all around it, the Robins shuttered and quickly started to deteriorate. Without proper heating and cooling, the

The auditorium of the Robins Theater as it appeared in 1987. *Courtesy of the* Warren Tribune.

old theater decayed under the stress of the elements. "There's been many occasions when people have wanted to go in there and restore the theater," Flaviano recalled. "But with all the changes downtown and all of the people gravitating toward the [Eastwood] Mall, it's been difficult." One of those attempts came in the late 1980s. KSB Enterprises acquired several buildings in the vicinity of the Robins. The old Gilmour's and Guarnieri Buildings were demolished, and the Robins and the former Ohio Theater/Duchess were scheduled for renovation. Contractors also removed the marquee from the Robins. Still, an active plan to fully renovate the theater and restore it to some productive use remained elusive.

In 2007, Heritage Ohio included the Robins on its list of "top preservation opportunities." A 2005 feasibility study estimated a cost of $12 million to fully renovate the building. Still, a lack of funding kept the theater sitting until 2014. That same year, a group, the Robins Project, sought to jump-start efforts to repurpose and renovate the building. Since then, it has begun working with organizations like the New School Urban Collaborative, attempting to place the theater's planned renovation within a larger effort to revitalize the downtown itself.

The Robins is one of the few theaters still standing in the Mahoning Valley, and it symbolizes a once-vibrant theater culture. Filmmaker Chris Columbus grew up in Warren before going on to write the screenplays for movies like *The Goonies* and *Gremlins* and directing such hits as *Home Alone* and two of the Harry Potter films. According to Columbus, "Warren, Ohio, did one important thing for me: it changed my life," he explained. "There was a theater called Daniel, downtown, where I would go every weekend. I think it was Robins and Daniels [*sic*], two theaters. And I would go every weekend and see a movie, and one weekend I went to see *Butch Cassidy and the Sundance Kid*. And that made me want to start making movies. I fell in love with moviemaking because of those theaters in Warren."[87] The Daniel today is a church, and the fate of the Robins remains uncertain. Preserving both theaters, in some form, would stand as a lasting memory to the city's long theater history—and to all whose lives it touched.

Part 5

THE GOLDEN AGE OF
THE DOWNTOWN MOVIE PALACES

THE STATE AND FORGOTTEN DOWNTOWN THEATERS

The names Palace, State, Warner and Paramount are readily recalled by Youngstowners who remember the 1940s through the 1970s. These theaters served as Youngstown's premier showcase picture houses; however, several other movie houses have since faded from collective memory. After the era of the nickelodeon waned, various theaters opened during World War I and throughout the 1920s. These often forgotten places provided a crucial niche for vaudeville lovers and moviegoers of the time.

The Hippodrome

One year after the Wilson Theater opened in 1914 on the east side of Youngstown, attention turned once again to the downtown. An enormous celebration took place on West Federal Street for the opening of the Hippodrome. Known as the "Hipp," the new vaudeville house excited the imagination of Youngstowners like no other theater before. Along with the Dome and, later, the Liberty, the Hippodrome was the second of three large theaters built within a short walking distance of West Federal and North Hazel Streets.

The Hippodrome's auditorium and stage were situated off Commerce Street, but the entrance to the building was located through a three-hundred-foot arcade on West Federal Street. Confectionery, millinery, music and jewelry stores were among the establishments situated inside. Its foyer contained thick carpeting to reduce sound and "retiring rooms," which came equipped with coat- and hat-check area. All of the rooms were finished in marble. The Hippodrome had a seating capacity of more than two thousand, making it the largest theater in the city.

An ivory, gold and rose color scheme predominated throughout the auditorium. The Hippodrome's large proscenium arch featured an elaborate latticework above it. Large private boxes graced either side of the stage, each capable of seating parties of eight. The theater's grand organ (absent for the opening due to wartime material shortages) contained enormous pipes that ran above the proscenium arch. The stage itself, designed to handle vaudeville productions and road shows, measured thirty-eight feet wide by thirty-one feet long. Electric announcing boards, a novelty at the time, informed audiences when each new act commenced. Publicity for the new theater repeatedly emphasized the role of everything from electric signage to electric dimmers inside the theater.

Beneath the stage, in the bowels of the theater, were twenty individual dressing rooms capable of accommodating sixty performers. The Hippodrome also included an animal room beneath the stage. Certain kinds of vaudeville productions utilized animals both big and small; dogs, monkeys, horses and elephants were housed and bathed in the animal room. Not long after the theater opened, a lion escaped from one of the rooms. A Hippodrome employee recalled the event: "It was just at noon, and you should have seen everybody run when that lion got loose. Two fellows were so excited that they both tried to get through a little door at the same time and got stuck. The lion was just as scared as we were, though."[88]

The Hippodrome hosted the Keith-Albee vaudeville circuit. Formed in the 1880s by Benjamin Franklin Keith and Edward Franklin Albee, the "Keith Circuit," as it was often called, existed to showcase "polite" vaudeville. Although American vaudeville was unique, the Keith-Albee circuit's focus on upstanding content reflected the original meaning of the French term *vaux de ville*, roughly translated as "worthy of the city's patronage." The Keith Circuit expanded with help from the Catholic Church, which supported the emphasis on morality that Keith and Albee espoused. By 1906, Keith-Albee had formed the United Booking Office. Under their terms, performers paid a commission to work in theaters controlled by the circuit.

It was the golden age of vaudeville, and the Hippodrome thrived during World War I and through the 1920s. Youngstown's own Rae Samuels played the Hippodrome on her way to national stardom, and Jack Benny, Buster Keaton and Victor Moore also graced the stage during the theater's heyday. At first, the theater showed two-a-day vaudeville performances in the afternoon and evening. Eventually, the schedule progressed to five and then eight acts per day, which amounted to about twelve total hours of vaudeville. Season ticket holders were common, usually attending on Tuesdays, Wednesdays, Thursdays and Saturdays. In 1922, the theater experimented with summer stock. Eventually, the Hippodrome adopted a mixed schedule, featuring motion pictures and vaudeville. Early admission prices were $0.50 for the afternoon and $1.65 for evening performances.

The Hippodrome's tenth anniversary was a gala affair; however, just one year later, the opening of the Palace Theater shifted the heart of local vaudeville to Central Square. After surviving the early Depression years, the Hippodrome underwent a complete renovation and reopened in 1934. Nevertheless, the theater closed one year later. The stage, a site of so many memorable shows, was demolished. A Greyhound bus station opened in its place, marking the symbolic end of Youngstown's long tradition of vaudeville.

The Capitol Theater

The Capitol Theater proved to be one of Youngstown's most ambitious and shortest-lived theaters. The architectural firm Stanley and Scheibel, which was involved with the construction of the Liberty Theater, designed the Capitol, which opened in 1922. The entire project cost an estimated $750,000, one of the most expensive theater projects in the Mahoning Valley up to that point. The auditorium provided seating for 1,400 guests and included a balcony. Box seating and an upscale mezzanine lounge advertised the theater as a first-class picture house, and a thirty-piece symphony orchestra added to the Capitol's distinguished offerings. Management purportedly acquired a Robert Morton pipe organ, something akin to what the Uptown Theater later featured, but it is unclear if it was ever installed. However, the theater did contain a Steinway Duo Art Grand Piano.

Charles Shutrump and Sons, a well-known local company, partnered with Youngstown businessman Carl F. Mogg to bankroll the project. It hired manager Charles Denzinger from the Strand Theater to run the Capitol. But despite planning, care and attention, the theater almost immediately faced financial difficulties. After only six months, the management of the Dome, which had taken over the theater, brought in Joseph Trunk to head

The ill-fated Capitol Theater opened for a brief time on East Federal Street during the 1920s. *Courtesy of Thomas Molocea.*

operations. Yet the Capitol never recovered, closing in 1923. First National Bank, and later Union National, occupied the building. A drugstore, fruit market and other assorted businesses later occupied the ground-floor premises. In 1969, all traces of the old Capitol disappeared under the wrecking ball. East Federal Street's most ambitious theater project melted into the past and faded from memory.

The Regent Theater

Over the years, downtown Youngstown came to be divided into two places. Central Square—or the "Diamond," as it was once called—delineated East Federal Street from the very different world of the west end of downtown. West Federal Street housed the most well-known clothiers, department stores and theaters, something that the ill-fated Capitol Theater had hoped to change. Delis, ethnic clubs and outdoor markets, where shoppers could even purchase live chickens, filled East Federal Street. A 1924 *Youngstown Vindicator* editorial contains some of the typical prejudices that shaped perceptions of the east end:

On the other side of the Square lies East Federal Street. For a few blocks the touch of America reaches, then—the other side of the melting pot is seen. Here is the pouring process; here is the teeming mass out of which comes West Federal Street. Its stores and shops speak English with a foreign accent. Clothing store windows ostentatious and ornate; jazz model suits, high peaked lapels, high button, wide bottom trousers, "Special" signs.... Here are also gingham dresses, heavy brogue and work shoes, overalls, cheap movie houses showing thrillers, cheap restaurants whose menus speak in Greek or Italian, or Spanish.[89]

One of those "cheap movie houses" was the Regent Theater, which opened around 1920. The Regent very much resembled a modern nickelodeon, with only the theater marquee to differentiate it from surrounding storefronts. The small theater could accommodate about 450 patrons, most of whom enjoyed a steady stream of early western and cowboy films throughout the 1920s, including *In the Days of Buffalo Bill*, the most popular film serial shown in the early years.

Pedestrians cross East Federal Street in front of the Regent Theater in the early 1960s. *Courtesy of Mark Peyko.*

The Regent was located close to several well-known black clubs; it primarily screened "race films" during the 1940s. *Courtesy of Mark Peyko.*

During the 1940s, the Regent became known as a favorite movie house for Youngstown's African American community. Outside the McGuffey Heights Theater in the Sharon Line neighborhood (owned by black businessman Roscoe Walker), only the Regent routinely served the community in a nondiscriminatory manner. At the time, an informal system of segregation dominated the city. Black patrons commonly found themselves relegated to the balcony area of most downtown theaters.[90] Managers did not hire black workers for positions such as usher or candy girl. Similar policies existed at restaurants and department stores.

It was East Federal Street where many African Americans went to shop and where black clubs and entertainment thrived. The Cleveland Bar, the Silver Dollar, the Sportere—which brought in national acts like Bill Doggett—and the Forty Club, located by the Regent, all lined the east end. The Regent also played films featuring live performances from the top black performers of the era. Thomas Rowe worked in janitorial services at the Palace Theater as a young man, and he ventured to the Regent to see concert films featuring his favorite artists. "The Regent showed many black movies," Rowe remembered. "They showed a lot of what you would call variety movies: Cab Calloway and his band live, Count Basie, appearing on stage, stuff like that. They also showed westerns and class B or C movies, but it was mainly there for black movies."

As a child, Liz Moore frequented the Regent regularly, but finding money for admission required some work. "It was twenty cents to get in," Moore explained. "And a bag of popcorn was ten cents. At the time, people drank pop out of bottles, and we'd go around fishing the old bottles out of trash cans. If you took them to the store, you got two cents for each one. That's how we made our movie money."

In his memoir *Dancing with Strangers*, Mel Watkins described a similar process:

> *And there were excursions by bike to Idora Park, where we rifled through refuse baskets to retrieve pop bottles and, though the practice was frowned upon, pedaled three miles back to Woodland [Avenue] and exchanged them for the two cents deposit they garnered at a local store. It was always a lucrative trip, one that financed the cost of refreshments and tickets for many Saturday afternoon jaunts to the Regent Theater—where customers were admitted and seated on a nondiscriminatory basis—or the Strand, where Negroes were permitted to sit in the first four rows.[91]*

In 1959, urban planners singled out East Federal as an area that "might be used for purposes other than the sale of shopper's goods."[92] Youngstown applied for federal assistance in 1964 to help finance three urban renewal projects, one of which included East Federal Street. Doomed, the Regent closed in 1966, and the property was folded into the east end urban renewal project; subsequently, most business establishments on East Federal were demolished. Today, it is almost impossible to imagine where the small movie house once stood.

The Cameo Theater

The Cameo began its life as the sister theater to the State, the latter of which opened in January 1928. The State's enormous success made the Cameo look like a sure bet; it wasn't. In a story similar to the Capitol's, the Cameo failed to find an audience during its brief life. But unlike the Capitol, the State's sister had two lives—one in the 1920s and the other in the 1930s.

While crowds continued to pack the State Theater in January, the Cameo opened across from the late Harry Burt's confectionery (now the Tyler

Mahoning Valley Historical Society) on West Federal Street. The movie house was designed mainly as a "dime theater." Prices at the State were thirty and forty cents for a matinee and upward of sixty cents for an evening show. The Cameo only charged ten cents for a matinee and twenty cents for an evening show. Audiences flocked to opening night, packing into the large auditorium. The Cameo became the third theater (behind the Palace and State) to open in downtown Youngstown in less than three years. Unlike its predecessors, it contained no stage and showed only motion pictures. The building also contained storefront shops, including the Cafaro Jewelry Company.

In sharp contrast to the discount theaters of today, the Cameo contained refinements common to a more elegant era of theater design. S.E. Trinkle of Trinkle Signs produced the posters and lobby displays. (Trinkle later worked on the Warner Theater.) The building featured a balcony capable of holding three hundred and a first-floor auditorium with seating for seven hundred patrons. The interior was finished in amber, with decorations in ivory and old gold. The lobby contained a sumptuous terrazzo floor; a George Kilgen and Sons organ provided accompaniment for the silent films. Ideally, the theater appealed to moviegoers looking for a bargain and an atmosphere of some elegance.

The management of the State controlled operations and saw its part of downtown as the beginning of "a new section of the city for amusements."[93] The Cameo primarily screened second-run films, featuring westerns with the likes of Tom Mix and Ken Maynard. But despite the management's best efforts, it faltered, closing before the end of 1928. The theater was revived and closed again on several occasions during the early Depression years, perhaps in an effort to catch budget-conscious moviegoers who avoided many of the larger, more expensive movie houses.

In the fall of 1937, the Cameo reopened after an extensive renovation. The theater's entrance was moved closer to the sidewalk, and several rows of seats were removed in order to expand the foyer. A restored terra-cotta façade glowed behind an enlarged marquee. The terrazzo floor remained, but a new color scheme consisting of Pompeian red, blue and silver transformed the interior. New projectors and a new screen were installed. Hand-woven silk fabrics covered the walls; new velour drapes separated the foyer and the auditorium. Citing the changing times, management adopted a regular program of "the unusual." *Slaves in Bondage*, an exploitation film about white slavery, headlined the opening program.

In a repeat of the theater's experience in the 1920s, the Cameo failed to reach audiences and closed in the early 1940s. The building next housed

Kirby Shoes, which had another location on East Federal Street. In 1959, the city demolished the old Cameo to make way for a parking lot, and the State's sister joined the ranks of the city's forgotten theaters.

The State Theater: From Movies to Music

Unlike its sister, the State enjoyed a long life as both a theater and a home to several live music venues. When construction commenced in the summer of 1927, the residents of Youngstown prepared themselves for the opening of the city's second large theater in as many years. The location already contained much theatrical history. In 1910, a nickelodeon owned by Klopot and Feinberg operated on the site of the future State; it later became known as the Nixon Theater. The Nixon gave way to the Orpheum, a small nickelodeon with a capacity of less than three hundred. However, the new State promised to greatly eclipse its predecessors and become the second-largest theater in the Mahoning Valley.

Forgotten in later years, the State was originally designed for both movies and vaudeville. The State was viewed as another house where both movies and live entertainment shared the stage, which was fairly common for large theaters built at that time. Newly elected mayor Joseph Heffernan, an enthusiastic vaudeville fan, volunteered to dedicate the new theater on opening night.

A bitterly cold winter day in early January 1928 failed to keep thousands of spectators from lining up outside the new theater. From West Federal Street, the State appeared to be quite narrow; the bulk of the building could be viewed best from West Boardman Street. A deep, vaulted façade distinguished it from surrounding storefronts.

Patrons entered the $500,000 theater through a promenade off West Federal Street and into a one-hundred-foot ivory- and gold-colored lobby. Two winding marble staircases off the foyer led to the mezzanine. Cut glass chandeliers elegantly hung in the lobby and the auditorium, which seated 2,100 patrons comfortably. The acoustics reflected the State's commitment to live shows, and several vaudeville performers, including the Four Serlaneys, a traveling variety group from Holland, appeared opening night. Dressing rooms were located adjacent to and below the stage. The State also included an orchestra pit and a Kimball organ (currently located in an Ontario, Canada church).

The theater changed rapidly in its early years. The State underwent its first redecorating in September 1928. After the first year of business, vaudeville

City buses pull up in front of the State Theater, circa 1967. *Courtesy of Mark Peyko.*

shows began to decline in importance. Management had planned to show one film daily and five acts of vaudeville; instead, live shows were phased out by the early 1930s.

The locally owned State soon ran into problems obtaining first-run films. Independent theater owners in the late 1920s found their businesses increasingly constrained by the limited number of films available to them. Subsequently, in 1930, Paramount-Publix, a theater division of Paramount Pictures, bought the State. At the time, all the major movie studios owned theaters, and Paramount-Publix operated three thousand nationwide in 1930. In downtown Youngstown, it also controlled the Cameo and Paramount.

All of the downtown movie houses suffered mightily during the Depression. The State was one of a few to actually close, at least temporarily, due to declining business. After it reopened, management attempted to introduce Bank Night—a first for any downtown theater. Every week, patrons enjoyed the chance to win fifty dollars during the Bank Night drawing. The Palace, Warner, Dome, Park and Strand eventually sued in common pleas court, claiming that the practice constituted "unfair competition." As the

Depression gradually subsided, the State regained its footing, unlike many neighborhood theaters, including the nearby Market Street and Ohio Theaters, both of which folded during the downturn.

By 1941, vaudeville was a thing of the past, but touring theatrical shows continued to come to the city during the 1940s, often to the Park Theater. At one time, live theater dominated the downtown, and a market for more stage productions seemed strong. The State's management decided to once again host live shows in 1941, after more than a decade of showing only films. The new policy of films and live productions began with *Life with Father* in November 1941. Yet fewer and fewer touring productions came through Youngstown as the decade progressed, and the State soon ended its new policy. After the Park Theater closed in 1948, Youngstown's grand tradition of hosting touring shows (with the exception of the Palace Theater) largely came to an end. The vibrant Youngstown Playhouse filled the community's needs for live theater from that point on.

The 1950s marked a decade of transition. In 1953, management introduced the first 3-D movies. The "golden era" of 3-D films began in the early 1950s and included movies such as *House of Wax*, *It Came from Outer Space* and *Creature from the Black Lagoon*. At the time, 3-D systems often used a polarized light method, which necessitated the wearing of cardboard glasses with polarizing filters. *Those Redheads from Seattle* premiered as the first film on the State's new thirty-eight-foot-wide panoramic screen. After the 3-D craze crested in 1954, financial problems forced the theater to shut down in the spring of 1955. A fruit market opened on the street in front of the building while it remained closed.

The State did not fully reopen on a consistent basis until 1957. Looking to better position the theater, management turned to major improvements to better compete with the other downtown movie houses as well as the ever-growing popularity of television. After adopting a reserved seat policy, the new State debuted in March 1957 as a "luxury theater." Redecorated and renovated, it featured a new curved screen capable of showing 70mm Todd-AO films. Six rows in the front of the theater were removed to accommodate the forty-seven-foot-wide screen; part of the balcony was also removed to give audiences a clear view of the larger screen. Seating capacity shrank commensurately to nine hundred, but the theater became more marketable than it had been prior to 1955—Youngstown was one of only thirty-five cities in the nation with Todd-AO.[94] Much like Hollywood, the theater's management hoped that new technology would allow it to better compete with television.

Despite their best efforts, the State, along with the rest of downtown's theaters, waned during the 1960s. In 1963, the Broumas chain took control of the theater. By then, competition had spread beyond the core of the city: the new Boardman and Lincoln Knolls Plaza cinemas catered to a rapidly expanding suburban clientele, and Wedgewood Cinema in Austintown Township opened in 1966, providing yet another outlet for these same moviegoers. The Broumas chain experienced massive financial problems over the next few years, and Youngstown Enterprises acquired the State in 1968.

In an effort to draw more business, the State began showing more controversial films as the Motion Picture Production Code, which enforced "moral guidelines" in filmmaking, ended in 1968. Films like *Candy* and, most notably, *I Am Curious (Yellow)* roused the ire of local censors. *I Am Curious (Yellow)*, a Swedish production that featured sex scenes and full-frontal male nudity, was one of the most controversial films of the late 1960s. After its debut at the State in 1969, police raided the theater, arrested projectionists and seized copies of the film. The State found itself immersed in a national controversy and an ensuing obscenity trial in Ohio.

The State, which featured a balcony, could seat 2,100 spectators. *Courtesy of Mahoning Valley Historical Society.*

Efforts to attract audiences to risqué art house films failed, and the State closed in 1970. In the wake of the theater's closing, a furniture store used the area underneath the stage for storage, precipitating a fire in 1972 that caused $100,000 in damages. In 1973, the Massullo family briefly reopened the old theater as the State Theater Hall of Music. They planned to feature an alternating mix of local and national rock acts every week. But it proved short-lived. The failure of the State Hall of Music appeared to doom any further prospects for hosting concerts at the old theater.

Contrary to expectations, a new music venue opened in the old State in October 1974. During its short life, the Tomorrow Club became famous throughout the Mahoning Valley. The group Focus played on opening night; KISS rocked the house days later. Considering Youngstown's declining economic fortunes during the mid-1970s, an incredible number of big acts and future rock legends played the Tomorrow Club. Ike and Tina Turner headlined the club, as did Heart, Rush, Boston, Meatloaf and Tom Petty. Management claimed that 150,000 people attended shows during the first nine months.[95]

"The Tomorrow Club had a lot of New Wave acts," Mark Peyko recollected. "The Talking Heads played there, Patti Smith, Blondie—many acts that became bigger later on. It would have been comparable to clubs on the East Coast. They were booking people at the same time, during the same era when those acts were playing at places like CBGB's and the Mudd Club in New York."

The Tomorrow Club also had memorable moments in punk rock. The Ramones played their first gig outside of New York City at the club in 1976.[96] They returned in 1978. (The group's signatures were still visible on a dressing room wall when the building was demolished.) In his memoir of life in the punk group the Pagans, Mike Hudson described playing the Tomorrow Club and meeting Stiv Bators (a Youngstown-area native) of the Dead Boys: "The Tomorrow Club was a huge old theater, run down but still elegant. The bill consisted of the Dead Boys, us and two Detroit bands, the Pigs and the Traitors. Madonna, then just some mousy looking girl from Michigan, was there as the girlfriend of one of the guys in the Detroit bands."[97] Such was the atmosphere of the club at the time.

Still, the Tomorrow Club closed at the end of 1978 after four brief years and was succeeded by the Agora. After a $200,000 renovation, the Youngstown Agora opened as part of a national chain that included thirteen clubs. Management restored the 2,100 original seats, making it the largest venue in the chain. But what it lacked was the support of the surrounding business community. Fights, vandalism and damaged storefronts frequently accompanied the end of shows. "Many places cause problems for the city," David Miller, president of the Youngstown Board of Trade, commented in 1982. "Unfortunately, the Agora name is used as a nomenclature for the total problem because they're the largest….I'm not sure that any big, empty building is good, but some businesses are detrimental."

Miller got his wish when the Agora closed in July 1982. After an aborted effort to turn the venue into a civic center, the old theater went dark again. It reopened as the Star Theater concert venue in 1984 but soon closed. Once again, it reopened in 1986 as the Star Palace. While the downtown around it transformed into a ghost town, the Star Palace hosted some of the top names in R&B and early hip-hop and provided a venue for up-and-coming local artists.

As a young woman, artist Candace "Candee Reign" Mauzy won a citywide talent contest at the Star Palace. The winner opened for national headliners at the venue. "You usually had twenty minutes to perform," Mauzy remembered. "I opened for Heavy D & the Boyz, Millie Jackson, Kool Moe Dee, Salt-N-Pepa, DJ Jazzy Jeff & the Fresh Prince and others. It was a wonderful experience. It was good for the community, and it kept us young people out of trouble."

Much like the Tomorrow Club and the Agora, the Star Palace closed after only a few years. The vacant State Theater sat in silence during the 1990s as downtown Youngstown rapidly deteriorated around it. By 2007, as an emerging revitalization movement gained steam in the old central business district, a small group of volunteers attempted to save the State from the wrecking ball. Then college student Jaime Hughes helped spearhead the effort.

"It was Christmas 2006, and my boyfriend and I passed the building one night on our way to Cedar's [Lounge], and we saw a for-sale sign on the State Theater building," Hughes explained. "The next day we called to see about the condition of the building." A group of people interested in saving the old State soon met to determine a course of action. However, the city had not secured the roof, which an individual had fallen through in the 1990s, and the theater languished in an advanced state of decay.

In 2008, the city demolished the old State; only the façade was saved. More than eight years later, the property still sits empty. Today, the fading façade reminds pedestrians of the last remains of one of the Mahoning Valley's most noteworthy entertainment establishments.

Palace Theater

For almost forty years, one of Mahoning Valley's most storied theaters stood at the heart of Central Square. The Palace Theater was, with the possible exception of the Warner, the most beautiful and palatial in the area. It began its life dedicated primarily to vaudeville, but long after variety shows vanished, some of the greatest names in music came to play on its stage, especially during the height of the big-band era. And the story of the Palace Theater's untimely fate in the 1960s is perhaps the most tragic in Youngstown's theatrical history.

Downtown Youngstown arguably reached its peak in the 1920s. Suburban sprawl was a thing of the future, and the central business district dominated Mahoning County as the center of retail and entertainment. "There was so much pedestrian traffic downtown," Youngstown resident Edward Manning remembered. "Dr. Joseph Wheeler, who was head of the public library, got the idea to put a branch library down on the central square....All the lodges

The Palace Theater was the jewel of Central Square for almost forty years. *Courtesy of Mark Peyko.*

and clubs were downtown....The doctors, dentists and lawyers were all downtown. A good many of the churches were on Wood Street and in the downtown section."[98]

In 1924, in the midst of this frenzied activity, developers announced that a new theater would be built on Central Square. The center of downtown had changed enormously since its early days as the "common." In 1870, the city dedicated the "man on the monument" Civil War statue on the square. The circus commonly came to town to perform in the same area, and the "Diamond block" of downtown businesses grew up around Central Square. In 1906, the city added a fountain, known as the "Maid," to Central Square. By 1925, all of that had changed: a branch library replaced the fountain, McCrory's replaced the Diamond block and construction had begun on the First National Bank Building and the new Keith-Albee Theater.

The Palace Realty Company planned to build a theater with attached office space at an estimated cost of $1 million. The building itself had frontage on three streets: 75 feet on Central Square, 105 feet on Wick Avenue and 75 feet on East Commerce Street. Retail space was available on the ground floor of the building. Local investors financed the building's construction, and the Keith-Albee vaudeville chain leased the theater. E.F. Albee himself sent a telegram to Youngstown on opening night in March 1926, wishing Youngstown well on its new endeavor: "I have built and managed many theaters in my time for the Keith-Albee circuit of vaudeville, and I can say without fear of contradiction that none are more perfect in all appointments or more beautiful."[99]

Thomas W. Lamb, one of the most noted theater architects in the world, designed the building. Lamb designed several theaters in Times Square, the Fox Theater in San Francisco and the B.F. Keith Memorial Theater, now the Boston Opera House. The Youngstown Keith, a neoclassical structure, matched the grandeur typical of a Keith-Albee theater: the interior featured white marble pillars, a large marble staircase and ornate plasterwork. Huge crystal chandeliers hung from the ceiling, and silk damask covered the lobby walls. The wrought-iron work on the grand staircase and along the mezzanine was done in bronze and iron. The mezzanine included an art gallery and silk-covered smoking lounges. The men's lounge featured a library, and both lounges contained marble fireplaces as centerpieces.

The auditorium was like nothing ever seen in the Mahoning Valley. It held seats for 2,300 patrons; a grand dome provided indirect lighting. The proscenium arch over the stage was done in a gold color, and a sculpture graced the uppermost part of the arch. The stage itself was fifty feet across and thirty-two feet deep. A large orchestra pit provided room for eighteen musicians. The twelve spacious dressing rooms were named after cities, with the "Youngstown Room" reserved for the biggest stars. A children's room served actors with young ones in tow, and a spacious greenroom was available for those looking to host guests or members of the media. Several of the dressing rooms contained baths; one featured a full kitchen. Baths were built to accommodate the animals that were often used in vaudeville productions, with room enough for large horses. After going backstage, performers had the option of traveling through an underground tunnel to get to their rooms at the nearby Tod Hotel.

Tickets for opening night sold for thirty-five cents for the balcony, fifty for the mezzanine, seventy-five for the orchestra and a dollar for loge seating. Patrons enjoyed a vaudeville show consisting of a fine pianist followed by burlesque routines featuring live gymnasts, a blackface sketch and a piece including live elephants, reindeers and ponies. The Greta Garbo film *Torrent* was the opening picture. The house ran on a schedule of three vaudeville shows a day plus silent films.

Famed manager Jack Elliott initially ran the Keith-Albee. Probably no one in the Mahoning Valley believed in vaudeville more than Elliott, and he above all was responsible for making Youngstown a prime spot for the best variety shows in the country. Elliot also hated motion pictures, which he considered inferior entertainment. His time at the theater was a constant struggle between the gradually fading world of live entertainment and the growing demand for films.

Elliott grew up in show business, from his youth in the circus to his days working at the Grand Opera House. He managed the Idora Park Theater and the Hippodrome during its early years, where he developed a skill for knowing which acts would succeed locally. Elliott brought the biggest names in the business to the Keith-Albee: Mae West, Joe E. Brown, Will Rogers and Eddie Cantor, among others. His tenure at the theater made it the vaudeville center of Mahoning Valley. The Keith hosted National Vaudeville Week in Youngstown every year during Elliott's reign; twenty-two acts played each day, and shows went past midnight.

The B.F. Keith Corporation merged in 1928 with the Orpheum vaudeville circuit, forming the Keith-Albee Orpheum Circuit, which subsequently merged into RKO (Radio-Keith-Orpheum). In 1929, RKO began aggressively promoting vaudeville. It controlled more than seven hundred theaters nationwide at the time. Jack Elliott declared "under this newly re-organized and rejuvenated system the entire machinery of scouting

The auditorium of the spacious Palace was typical for the design of a Keith-Albee theater. *Courtesy of Mahoning Valley Historical Society.*

for new talent and new material, for developing and presenting attractions, for booking the endless chain of modern theaters, has been adjusted."[100]

Elliott and RKO's promised new era of vaudeville did not arrive, however. Instead, talkies and the Great Depression took their toll on the theater's live shows and on the Keith itself, which became known as the B.F. Keith Palace in 1929. In May 1932, management announced the end of vaudeville shows. Under the new policy, only films were to be shown. Yet only two months later, after ongoing financial problems, the Keith closed entirely. The theater reopened again in September 1932 with Jack Elliott at the helm but once again closed in May 1933.

Theater man Ed Prinsen, with several partners, stepped in to try and save the Keith Palace. By 1933, Prinsen had already enjoyed a long career. He started out selling film for Paramount Pictures and eventually ran the State, Paramount and Cameo Theaters in Youngstown for Paramount-Publix. Prinsen and partners formed the Public Square Theater Company in 1933 with the express purpose of revitalizing the Palace.

A plan was arranged between Prinsen and partners and Dollar Bank, which owned the mortgage: the bank would receive a percentage of the box office in lieu of rent. The Palace Theater (as it was henceforth called) hosted a grand reopening in September 1933. Katharine Hepburn and Douglas Fairbanks starred in the opening night's film, *Morning Glory*. Vaudeville returned as part of the theater's new "balanced policy" of motion pictures and live shows.

Throughout most of the Depression, vaudeville, though diminished, continued. Professor Donald Elser recalled the theater scene in downtown Youngstown during the Depression: "There were at that time, at least seven or eight motion picture shows running all the time. They had a live show at the Palace during the day and a live show at the Hippodrome at times, and then the old Park Theater down on East Federal ran what they called vaudeville. This was second grade, third grade vaudeville and a movie for something like thirty cents."[101] After the Hippodrome closed in 1935, some form of vaudeville continued at the Palace until about 1942. However, live entertainment on the theater's stage did not end. Instead, the era of the big bands revitalized the live offerings as America prepared for war.

The rise of swing music in the 1930s and the subsequent birth of the big bands electrified ballrooms throughout the nation. In Youngstown, the Idora and Elms Ballrooms and the Mansion—a popular dance club located on the former H.K. Wick estate on Logan Road—swung every week to the melodies of popular youth music. The city's central location between Chicago and New York, and between Pittsburgh and Cleveland, made it a prime attraction for national touring groups. As vaudeville faded away, the Palace, with its large stage, became a stopping point for the bands of the era: Vaughn Monroe, Hal McIntyre, Jimmy Dorsey, the Andrews Sisters and many others played the Palace during the swing era.

No one epitomized the big-band era more than Glenn Miller and his orchestra. Miller was mobbed and the suit nearly torn from his body when he played the Yankee Lake Ballroom for 4,200 fans in 1941. He performed at the Palace for three days in August 1942. Only months earlier, he received a gold record for the song "Chattanooga Choo-Choo." The Miller orchestra played five shows a day at the Palace, two of which were broadcast nationally.

William FitzGerald of the *Youngstown Vindicator* wrote at the time, "People passing the Palace Theater yesterday must have been startled to hear waves of cheering and yelling from the auditorium. It was Youngstown—with the accent on young—greeting Glenn Miller and his Chesterfield orchestra on the stage. And Miller, suave as ever, responded with 45 minutes of smooth entertainment which had the kids screaming for more. Every number his band played seemed to send shivers of ecstasy through the house."[102]

August 1942 proved to be one of the Palace's most memorable months. Frank Sinatra came to town for what turned out to be one of his last shows with the Tommy Dorsey Orchestra. In 1939, *Metronome* magazine featured a review of the "very pleasing vocals of Frank Sinatra, whose easy phrasing is especially commendable."[103] Less than a year later, he was making records with Tommy Dorsey, one of the top bandleaders in the business. In November 1941, Sinatra sang at the Palace for the first time with Dorsey. He was not the headliner, but audiences lit up as soon as he walked on stage. By the summer of 1942, Sinatra was looking for a way to get out of his contract and move on to a solo career.

He and Dorsey returned to the Palace in late August for a three-night engagement, with five shows each day. The first night's performance was broadcast live on the *Tommy Dorsey Show*. Sinatra sang "Just as Though You Were Here," and Dorsey played his famous "Intermezzo." The final show went out live across the nation. Yet all was not well; some in the audience later reported that Sinatra announced his desire to go solo that night.[104] In any event, Sinatra went out on his own only days later—beginning his rise to the status of music legend.

When stars like Sinatra came to the theater, they usually dined at the Palace Grill, one of several businesses that occupied storefronts on the ground level of the building. Originally, the Palace Restaurant served as the premier business attraction; it later gave way to Friedman's Confectionary, which in turn became Sweetland, another confectionery. Sweetland attracted movie patrons and students looking for a diversion during daytime classes. "I went there when I was an undergraduate at Youngstown College," Fred Posey recalled. "Some of us [students] would go down there and get a milkshake, made with a real egg, at lunch time."

The Palace complex also included offices. Well-known performer and vocal coach Grace Straw Wilson rented space in the building. Wilson began performing at the age of four and studied under some of the most prominent vocal coaches in the country. Richard Scarsella later recalled the atmosphere inside the building at the time. "I took singing lessons there at the theater," Scarsella explained. "I'd be in the studio warming up, and I could hear the movie coming in faintly through the wall."

During the 1950s, the Palace represented one of the "big four theaters" downtown, which included the Paramount, State and Warner. Going downtown to a movie usually involved a special occasion and a certain wardrobe, according to Bill DeCicco. "You could probably go to the Newport, Foster, the Uptown, or some place like that, with your friends. But there was sort of a stigma: you didn't go to one of the downtown theaters like the Palace—especially on a Friday or Saturday night—unless you had a date," he emphasized. "You can see photos of people standing in line on the street with a suit and a tie on, and those were high school kids, too."

Live shows continued on the Palace's stage during the 1950s. The occasional burlesque star came to the theater—usually one of the biggest names, like Gypsy Rose Lee. Patti Page performed in 1951 on the heels of her huge hit "Tennessee Waltz." Comedians played the Palace as well, including the Three Stooges. And Larry Steele's "Smart Affairs," the largest black entertainment touring show in the country, performed for packed houses. *The Country Girl, Guys and Dolls, South Pacific* and other Broadway touring shows continued to visit the Palace, one of the very last venues in Youngstown capable of handling such productions in the 1950s. However, the popularity of television gradually eroded the viability of live shows; movies almost exclusively dominated by the end of the decade.

Troubling economic changes threatened the central business district and the Palace itself by the end of the 1950s: retail establishments were leaving for the suburbs; ridership on the local bus system declined; and retail sales, while continuing to grow in the city at large, remained stagnant for downtown businesses.[105] The downtown theaters suffered from a perceived lack of available parking, and business for evening shows dropped off as early as 1951. A 1963 report on Youngstown and nine other similar metropolitan areas found that the city's downtown suffered the greatest loss in sales of any city studied.[106] All of these factors subsequently affected the Palace, State, Warner, Regent and Strand.

In the summer of 1962, Ed Prinsen died after years as the head of operations at the Palace. Robins Enterprises took over the theater until Broumas Theaters acquired it in June 1963. William Petrych, one of the most ubiquitous faces in the local theater business, took over as manager. At the time, the Palace joined the State, Newport, Liberty Plaza, Lincoln Knolls and the Boardman Plaza Cinema as part of the local Broumas chain. In late 1964, Broumas announced the closing of the Palace. Almost immediately, the area's best-known theater entrepreneur sensed an opportunity.

Ever since he reacquired the Newport Theater after a temporary semi-retirement, Peter Wellman had hoped to once again compete with the downtown theaters. This dream of his dated back to the 1940s. In 1948, Wellman built the palatial Belmont Theater on Belmont Avenue in

The Palace closed in 1964 and two years later was demolished to make way for an aborted mall project. *Courtesy of Thomas Molocea.*

Youngstown. The *Youngstown Vindicator* referred to it as "one of the finest neighborhood houses ever built in Ohio."[107] With all the comfort and class of a downtown movie house and plenty of readily available parking, the Belmont posed a threat to the central business district's theaters, most of which tried to stifle Wellman's efforts to secure first-run films. After a struggle, the Belmont ignominiously closed in the 1950s, becoming an Atlantic Mills discount store.

In 1964, Wellman had a chance to actually own a downtown theater. Bob Vargo, then an employee, discussed the possibility of acquiring the Palace with Wellman at the time. "Wellman asked me if I thought we could do anything with the theater," Vargo recalled. "I said to him, you have a great stage. You have all of the office space upstairs and only half is rented out. If you get it, all of the people in there now can stay, and we could get more tenants to cover our costs." And according to Vargo, John Kenley of the well-known Kenley Players was interested in the possibility of doing summer stock on the Palace's stage.

However, it was Stephen C. Baytos, a shopping center developer, who acquired the old theater. Baytos grew up in Youngstown and began building houses in suburban Boardman. By 1964, he had built more than fifty different shopping centers across the country and was responsible for the Voyager Motor Inn in downtown Youngstown in 1963. Baytos envisioned building a $3 million mall along with a 1,200-seat Cinerama Theater dubbed the New Palace Theater. The plans included ground-floor parking, forty-five apartments and a "moving sidewalk" to bring customers up from the lobby floor. A lounge and restaurant were planned for the third floor. He dubbed the ambitious project "Plaza I." Simultaneously, he planned to build the Legal Arts Center on the site of the old Sears building.

Baytos named John Broumas as the manager of the proposed New Palace. Addressing the outrage that many expressed over the demolition of the old Palace Theater, Broumas replied, "In the days when theaters such as the Palace were built, they were designed as real showplaces because it was a place to enjoy. This has changed. And people come to see the show, then go home or to a restaurant. They don't sit around and talk in the lobby or admire the paintings and other decorations."

Mayor Anthony B. Flask told the city council that the Legal Arts Center and Plaza I represented "the most startling development in the city in fifty years."[108] However, in August 1965, Baytos announced that the project was on hold through 1970 due to a tenant's refusal to leave before his lease ended in 1966. Plaza I never materialized, but the wrecking ball did put an end to the Palace in the summer of 1966. Demolition took longer than expected due to the incredible construction of the building.

In 1969, the People's Bank of Youngstown bought the site from Baytos in order to build an office building, which became another aborted project. In 1970, the Dale-Howe Corporation proposed building a $7.5 million, seventeen-story "motor inn" containing two hundred rooms on the site. The project never left the drawing board. Instead, the old Palace site became a parking lot, which it remains now, fifty years later. To this day, those who remember the theater mourn the needless destruction of one of the city's most beautiful and storied structures.

Not all traces of the Palace are lost. In September 1965, the Palace's interior furnishings were put up for auction. Buyers could purchase the sconces, paintings, the marquee, the box office, chandeliers and even the red carpet. All of the old theater's fineries scattered to the four winds. Yet decades later, the pipe organ reemerged in Boardman. In 2010, after ten years of work, master organ builder Vic Marsilio successfully restored the Wurlitzer Style H Special organ. Today, it is housed at C&C Ribbon on South Avenue. To hear it is to be temporarily transported back to a long-lost era of theater history, one thick with memories. And memories are all that is left, for the old organ is now the last physical connection to what many consider the finest movie palace ever built in Mahoning Valley.

WARNER THEATER

If one theater rivaled the Palace as Mahoning Valley's most beautiful, it was the Warner. Dedicated to the memory of Sam Warner, the movie house symbolized Youngstown at its height and capped the last great building boom downtown. Nevertheless, it had the shortest lifespan of any of the "big four" theaters. Yet of all the downtown theaters, only the Warner escaped the wrecking ball. Today, it lives on as Powers Auditorium, one of Ohio's premier venues for live productions.

In April 1925, David Warner arrived in Youngstown representing Warner Brothers Pictures, Incorporated. He announced that a new Warner Theater would be erected between Chestnut and Hazel Streets for an estimated $750,000. Architects arrived to examine the proposed site, and negotiations began to acquire the land. Despite the news, nothing immediately happened. Two years later, Sam Warner died unexpectedly at the age of forty. According to Bob Vargo, "After Sam died, the other Warner brothers began looking in New Castle for a place to build a theater to honor their late brother. When word got out that they were looking to build a theater, all of the property prices shot up." Subsequently, the plans for the proposed theater shifted back to Youngstown.

Shortly after the onset of the Great Depression, after several years of delays, the Warner Theater project finally commenced near the corner of West Federal and North Chestnut Streets. That particular corner had already witnessed a great deal of history. The original town hall once stood on this site, and the Warner brothers themselves lived just up the street as youths. Prohibition brought the Cornfield Club to the block during the 1920s. According to rumor, the club contained a large barrel-like structure in the basement where liquor could be quickly dumped in the event of a raid. After contractors demolished the Cornfield to make way for the Warner, they discovered the structure, but much to the dismay of the men, it contained no liquor. A longtime hotel also fell to make way for the theater, but Warner Brothers planned a new and more ambitious one to replace it.

They envisioned a twenty-story hotel immediately adjacent to the theater. For unknown reasons—possibly because frontage on West Federal Street was going for as high as $10,000 per front foot—Warner Brothers never acquired the requisite land. If the project had gone forward, the hotel would have been the tallest building downtown.

Construction on the Warner proceeded as planned, but not without delays. The city did everything to guarantee that the company hired local workers for the project. Yet tremendous conflicts roiled the labor market during the 1930s, and a dispute emerged among carpenters, bricklayers and the general contractor over proposed reductions in wages. Failing to come to an agreement, work halted for a month during the summer of 1930. The head of the studio's construction department filed a letter of protest with the city, and an agreement was finally reached to get the project back on schedule.

The architectural firm Rapp and Rapp, responsible for the Oriental and Palace Theaters in Chicago and the Paramount Theater in Times Square, designed the Warner. The firm designed the façade in the Art Moderne style, later altered to reflect a more Modernist style. Much like the nearby Paramount Theater, the Warner showcased a large vertical blade sign that could be seen far down West Federal Street.

The exotic and expensive materials used in the Warner's construction made it perhaps the most unique project of its kind in Mahoning Valley history. Heller Brothers contractors brought the project to fruition for $1.5 million, much higher than the 1925 estimate of $750,000. No expense was spared. Only the finest and often extremely rare woods were selected for the interior paneling: Italian olive wood, Australian and African cherry, Carpathian elm, Macassar ebony and English walnut. Contractors used many rare woods, making them extremely difficult to replace during renovations in later years.

The finest craftsmen worked on the Warner's hand-molded plasterwork. Arthur Buttner, a graduate of the Royal College of Arts in London, came to Youngstown to fashion the interior ornamentation. He had previously labored on the Oriental Theater in Chicago and the Fox Theater in Detroit. For six months, Buttner designed the Warner's twenty-foot-high Spanish dancers, animals and masks. The artist also worked on the proscenium canopy over the stage using model figures from which he painstakingly cast the final product.

Elegance and attention to detail defined the rest of the interior. Large gold-plated mirrors covered both sides of the ninety-foot-long lobby, bearing a resemblance to the Versailles Hall of Mirrors. Crystal chandeliers and

The interior of the Warner represented the pinnacle of design and craftsmanship. *Courtesy of the* Warren Tribune.

marble pilasters added to the royally luxurious atmosphere. Red, gold and silver color schemes predominated in the tapestries, panels and tiles. One of the theater's more exotic elements was the Spanish/Moorish patio immediately adjacent to the lobby. A blue dome above symbolized the sky under which a fountain was showcased by beautifully colored Mexican tile. The feel of the space suggested an outdoor Mediterranean setting. The original concession area was located in the patio, and a staircase led from there to the mezzanine. On the far end of the grand lobby, another marble staircase, with railings of solid bronze, also led to the mezzanine.

Smoking and lounge suites for men and women were situated off the main lobby and on the second floor. *Town Talk* magazine, a local publication that covered society happenings, business and culture, described the lower lounge room before the opening: "This room is one of the most beautiful and unusual in all theaterdom. It is reached down a wide winding staircase, which leads you into this large oval room with its large inviting fireplace in the south end. Large round pillars of Macassar ebony reach in their dignity and beauty to the domed ceiling. The room is beautifully paneled in rare, especially selected Carpathian elm and Italian olive wood with trim of Australian cherry and English walnut."[109] For entertainment, the main lounge featured a Brunswick Automatic Panatrope capable of playing twenty different records in a row. Drinking fountains emblazoned with the slogan "Drink and be refreshed" were available outside both sets of lounges.

The auditorium itself reflected the Spanish influence of the patio room with the addition of elaborate rococo ornamentation; hundreds of yards of specially woven orange satin and tussah silk tapestries graced the walls. Originally, four large picture-frame openings above the proscenium arch were to house portraits of the Warner brothers. After technical issues necessitated using two of the openings for sound projection, the company decided against the idea. The forty-foot Magnascope screen represented an early effort at widescreen projection. During select scenes, the projectionist would use a specially designed lens to enlarge the image, thus cropping off the top and bottom part of the frame.

With well over 2,500 seats, the Warner's auditorium became the largest in Mahoning Valley. Six main aisles led to the 2,000 floor seats, and the balcony was cantilevered to prevent obstructed views. In order to test the strength of the twelve-foot-high girders supporting the balcony, engineers used sandbags to imitate the weight of a capacity audience. The plush blue leather seats were designed with the utmost comfort in mind.

The behind-the-scenes aspects of the theater proved equally as impressive. The building contained 113 rooms, not including office space. Ushers had their own changing rooms and showers. Although the Warner never hosted regular stage performances, the theater did contain small dressing rooms. Even the projectionist had a special lavatory and shower. Staff communicated with the projectionist and others in the vast building using an automatic telephone exchange. An enormous ventilating system "washed" the air in the theater, and a maze of 325,000 feet of copper wire and 63,000 feet of steel conduit pipe made electricity possible. Workers installed more than 6,200 lamp sockets, some of which powered $1,000 decorative lamps. The building's power plant was capable of lighting 2,500 typical-sized homes.

By May 1931, the grand jewel of downtown was ready for its close-up. Opening night was like no other in the history of Mahoning Valley theater culture. Days before the opening, business owners on West Federal Street decorated their storefronts in preparation for the premiere. In the hours before the opening, a brass band played for growing crowds of onlookers. Klieg lights lit up the sky at dusk, and a traffic jam all but shut down the streets. Vehicles disgorged prominent couples dressed in formal attire, many

Local artist Arthur "Barney" Carnes designed the program for the opening of the Warner Theater in Youngstown. *Courtesy of Thomas Molocea.*

preening for the cameras. Youngstown Sheet and Tube president Frank Purnell was on hand, as was former president James Campbell. A *Youngstown Vindicator* reporter remarked, "You'd never have believed had you been a Buck Rogers, returning from a trip to Mars, that Mother Earth was in pains of a Depression. The gowns in which feminine beauty whisked to the new Warner would indicate they had the treasuries of kingdoms at their command."[110]

Couples inside greeted theater manager and Warner family brother-in-law David Robins, accompanied by Mrs. Robins, formerly Annie Warner. Male and female "mannequins," dressed to the nines, mingled with guests while movie cameras recorded it all. A Duo-Art Reproducing Piano played on the balcony of the grand staircase. Mayor Joseph L. Heffernan, dressed in swallowtails, prepared for his speech. He had laid the cornerstone for the theater only three months before.

Once onstage, the mayor greeted the crowd with a pro-Youngstown speech intended to cement the city as having "arrived": "I never thought the time would come when we would see in West Federal Street a building like this....It's a tribute of the Warner Brothers to their faith in the future of our home city. They're businessmen, but this building would not have been created but for the sentimental attachment of the Warner brothers for Youngstown." After paying further tribute to the Warner brothers, he acknowledged the Depression raging in the city and country outside: "Let us forget our troubles and move forward to a glorious future—heart to heart and shoulder to shoulder."[111]

The night's program included the playing of the Wurlitzer Style 240 organ followed by various singers. Albert S. Howson, representing Warner Brothers, spoke, and the mayor crowned Miss Catherine Corbett "Miss Warner." He then presented a bronze plaque to Howson to commemorate the occasion. The night's film was *The Millionaire*. Written by Broadway playwright Earl Derr Biggers, a native of Warren, it proved a fitting finale for the evening.

The opening of the Warner Theater truly symbolized Youngstown at its historic height. Only thirty years earlier, West Federal Street and the downtown still featured homes and horses, far from the commercial center it had become by 1931. The city's population increased from about 44,000 to 170,000 during that same period. The economic prosperity brought by the steel industry contributed to a building boom. During the 1920s alone, downtown saw an addition to the YMCA; the building of Central Tower, McCrory's, the Central Square branch of the library, First Baptist Temple and Central Square Garage; the State, Palace and Capitol Theaters; Strouss Hirshberg's; the Union National Bank; and the joining of two separate buildings to form McKelvey's.

Businesses near the Warner greatly benefited from West Federal Street's newest addition. Just three doors to the east, a new A&P grocery store opened. Rainbow Lunch, a popular eatery known for its barbecue sandwiches, was right next door. The prestigious Manhattan Restaurant operated nearby, and Shy Lockson Tailors, one of the most notable tailors in the city, eventually opened in the Warner building. A Turkish bath was located adjacent to the theater, and the Theater Bar opened to service patrons after the Warner's evening shows.

Despite the euphoria over the new Warner, the Depression still gripped the city in the early 1930s. By 1932, economic conditions had rapidly deteriorated. In May of that year, the *Atlantic Monthly* spotlighted Youngstown, then known as "the hungry city." Mayor Heffernan described conditions in the city's incinerator building and an abandoned police station, where scores of men huddled daily for shelter and warmth: "There were old men gnarled by heavy labor, young mechanics tasting the first bitterness of defeat, clerks and white-collar workers learning the equality of misery, derelicts who fared no worse in bad times than in good…each one a personal tragedy and all together an overwhelming catastrophe for the Nation."[112]

The theater business suffered mightily under such conditions. Just two months after the *Atlantic* article, the Keith-Albee closed downtown, and rumor had it the Warner, only a year after opening, would also soon close. The Warner narrowly survived the Depression, unlike the nearby Dome Theater, which permanently shuttered in 1936.

Despite the Depression, Warner Brothers proposed building another Youngstown theater. In early 1940, the company bought property on the east side of Elm Street between Broadway and Bissell Avenues on the north side. According to Nat Wolf, manager of the Cleveland division, the new Warner would occupy the site where Ben and Pearl Warner once lived. The company planned for a one-thousand-seat auditorium with the most modern of amenities.[113] It would have been the first theater located on the north side of Youngstown, but for unknown reasons, construction never began.

The dawning of the 1940s brought crowds of shoppers and moviegoers back to downtown Youngstown. Well-dressed women and men, even those who lived in the suburbs, came to the central business district for most of their shopping needs. More and more cars began to appear on downtown streets as well, especially after the end of World War II, filling parking lots as far away as Lincoln Avenue during the Christmas shopping season. The parking problem presented an issue for movie houses, yet theaters attracted the majority of the nighttime retail traffic downtown.

In 1941, David Robins died and was replaced by Frank Savage, who continued to run the theater for the next two decades. *Youngstown Vindicator* theater critic Fred Childress described the Warner as "the place to go" during the 1930s and 1940s. According to him, "It had the pick of most of the Hollywood movies, from *Gone with the Wind* to *Wuthering Heights*, and continued to have them until 1949, when government antitrust suits forced an end to such practices."[114]

Prior to 1949, the major studios had their own theater chains. Additionally, they used "block booking," which forced independent theater owners to sign contracts guaranteeing that they would exhibit certain blocks of studio films. The government gradually targeted this system, arguing that it monopolized first-run movies—as well as actors and actresses, who were often bound to particular studios by long-term contracts. After the 1948 decision *U.S. v. Paramount Pictures, et al.*, the big Hollywood studios divested themselves of their chains, which directly affected the Warner Theater, and as a result, Warner Brothers sold its interest to the Stanley Warner Corporation in 1952.

During the 1950s, the Warner featured such hits as *A Star Is Born*, with Judy Garland; *Young at Heart*, starring Frank Sinatra and Doris Day; and *Rio Bravo* with John Wayne, Dean Martin and Ricky Nelson.

Disaster nearly struck in 1959 when a fire broke out at nearby Hume's Furniture. The initial blaze quickly spread to three different buildings. Automatic fire doors prevented the inferno from becoming uncontrollable, but power was cut to the Warner when officials feared it might reach the theater. Yet it was not fire but economic and cultural changes that ultimately threatened the future of the Warner.

The Warner Theater, circa 1957. *Courtesy of Thomas Molocea.*

The closing of the Palace Theater in 1964 sent shockwaves through the downtown. It was only the first domino to fall. Suburbanization and the rise of the local drive-ins and plaza theaters took their toll during the early part of the decade, and noticeably, the Warner looked shabby and unkempt by the late 1960s. The ceiling deteriorated to the point where a giant piece of plaster fell one night after closing, destroying nearly thirty seats.[115] Still, few were prepared for the incredible news in early 1968 that the Warner would soon close.

A capacity crowd streamed in to say goodbye to the jewel of West Federal Street in February 1968. *Bonnie and Clyde*, starring Warren Beatty and Faye Dunaway, closed out the last week. So many people bought tickets that the theater oversold for the first time ever. Manager Marie Wollitz, who helped open the theater in 1931 as a cashier, greeted customers. One man mentioned to Wollitz that he hadn't attended a show at the Warner in years. "That's one of the reasons it is being closed," she replied.[116] The Glen Alden Corporation allowed employees to be transferred elsewhere, but the fate of the theater itself appeared far less certain.

No firm plans immediately existed for the Warner's future, but the organ and ticket booth were sold. By the end of summer, several plans had been floated for the old Warner: converting it into a discount store, creating a theater and convention hall through the city's urban renewal program or turning it into a parking lot. In early September, Binama Realty Company announced that it would raze the Warner's auditorium and convert the area into parking. The old lobby would become an arcade. A Cleveland parking firm quickly began negotiating for the space, and an auction of the theater's fixtures was planned for late September. A *Youngstown Vindicator* editorial announced, "The Warner Dies."[117]

Just when it looked like it would share the destiny of the Palace, fate intervened. Stockbroker Edward Powers and his wife, Alice, happened to be watching television one night when they saw a story about the Warner's impending demolition, scheduled for early December 1968. They immediately decided to get involved. According to Bob Vargo, "Alice postulated that the Youngstown Symphony, then playing at Stambaugh Auditorium, could have a full-time home at the Warner. The bank assumed that Powers would never be serious enough to make the deal, but he ponied up the $250,000 to save the historical structure at the very last minute."

The money allowed the Youngstown Symphony to take control of the old theater. It then campaigned to raise an additional $350,000 in order to fully rehabilitate it. Longtime local manager Jack Hynes was brought in to help lead the charge. He later remembered the many problems the aged theater faced:

> *When we came in here, we found a theater that was structurally sound but in need of a great deal of rehabilitation. For example, the carpets had big holes in them. They were ripped and pulled apart. The seats were cut. The water pressure in the building was so poor that if you flushed the toilets you couldn't get a drink of water. The lighting equipment had deteriorated to such an extent that we had ten-watt bulbs in the outside marquee, and when you put twenty-five watt bulbs in, the whole thing blew out.*

Members of the local painters' union volunteered their time on the renovation. Skilled craftsmen from Italy repaired the rococo plaster ornamentation that had sustained water damage from a leaky roof. Workers replaced the old seats in the auditorium and more than 3,200 yards of carpeting; a general cleaning of everything in the theater commenced. The Youngstown Symphony Society initially estimated the cost of refurbishing the theater into a suitable performance venue at $170 a seat.

Jack Hynes, former manager of the Park and Paramount Theaters, was involved in transitioning the old Warner to Powers Auditorium. *Courtesy of the* Warren Tribune.

Members of the Youngstown Symphony pose for a group photo inside Powers Auditorium. *Courtesy of the* Warren Tribune.

In order to fully convert the old theater, the orchestra pit was enlarged and the stage extended ten feet, which reduced the seating capacity to 2,300. The inadequate stage dressing rooms also had to expand. Large petals were added to the ceiling, along with side acoustic panels, to accommodate the theater's new purpose: ballet, opera, music and live theater.

The Youngstown Symphony's new home, Powers Auditorium, became a rare success story in the annals of saving and repurposing local theaters. Today, Powers is part of the DeYor Performing Arts Center, which also encompasses the six-hundred-seat Ford Family Recital Hall. Overture, an attached restaurant, is open during performances and serves lunch to the public during weekdays. Outside on West Federal Street, a plaque commemorates the old theater, reminding younger generations of the Warner's place in film history and its connection to the life and times of the Warner family and their film empire.

Part 6

A NEW FRONTIER

Drive-Ins and Beyond

By the beginning of the 1970s, the golden age of downtown movie houses had ended. At one time, at least eight theaters operated simultaneously in Youngstown's central business district; Warren boasted four. None remained opened by the bicentennial. The theater business began to expand beyond the downtown and urban neighborhood as early as the 1940s: the new drive-in theaters and later the plaza and mall cinemas transformed the landscape. As the conveniently located neighborhood theaters vanished, cinemas opened in plazas and malls, which usually required driving. One-stop shopping and a movie downtown became one-stop shopping and a movie in the suburbs.

The drive-in marked the first postwar evolution in movie going. According to historian Kerry Segrave, "Along with the pioneering shopping malls, drive-ins led the post–World War II rush to suburbia. Both catered to families who didn't want to return to the city at night—it was too much of a hassle. But these families were ready to drive to a mall or a drive-in."[118] The first drive-in opened in Camden, New Jersey, in 1933, but it took until the end of the war before the new trend exploded across the country. Between the end of World War II and 1953, more than 850 traditional theaters opened; more than 4,500 closed during the same period. Nearly 3,000 drive-ins opened during that time span; only 342 closed.[119]

During this period, drive-ins arrived in the Mahoning Valley. The first to open is nearly forgotten today. The Outdoor Auto Theater, like many of the early drive-ins, sported a simple name and an even simpler setup. Located outside of Youngstown on Route 62, it opened in the summer of 1940. Theater owner Donald Hegfield described it as "just a couple of sticks sticking up with a screen." With no snack bar and few other amenities, the Outdoor Theater lasted only a few years.

In 1947, Peter Wellman opened the Youngstown Drive-In (later called the Southside Drive-In) in an undeveloped section of Boardman. This new "ozoner," as early dive-ins were called, properly introduced Mahoning Valley to movies under the stars. The theater could accommodate seven hundred cars and showed two films nightly, with a special midnight show on Saturdays. A sixty-foot screen with neon towers greeted the carloads of families arriving for opening night's film, *The Courage of Lassie*. All children were admitted free; the theater featured a bottle warming service for young mothers.

One month later, the Sky-Hi Drive-In opened on forty acres in Coitsville Township. Smaller than the Southside, the outdoor theater accommodated a maximum of 620 cars. The large screen (billed as "a giant steel picture tower") was fifty feet wide. In the 1950s, management installed outdoor heaters, allowing the drive-in to operate the entire year. Similar to the small speakers that provided sound to each car, patrons attached an individual heater to their window. Many drive-ins across the country had such heaters: some, like the Sky-Hi, were attached to posts; at other theaters, they were handed out individually at the concession area. The Sky-Hi and Elm Road remained the only local drive-ins to stay open year-round.

In his autobiography, *Running with God*, Patrick DiCicco described going to the Sky-Hi on winter nights during the early 1960s: "It was open year round, and it wasn't unusual to go there in the winter, as they had portable heaters that you put in your window with your speaker. On nights that I couldn't see Marcia, me and the guys would sneak our friends into the drive-in in the trunks of our cars, then pop the back seat and let them out when we parked. It didn't matter if it was snowing or not, it was a good place to hang out and make-out."[120]

Drive-ins attracted car-crazy youths during the 1950s and 1960s. The nickname "ozoners" often gave way to the term "passion pits," as many drive-ins came to be called. In the privacy of their own car, hormonal teens found the outdoor theaters far more amenable to the art of "necking." Drive-ins also changed their offerings accordingly, from more family-friendly fare

Left: For nearly forty years, the Sky-Hi Drive-In in Coitsville attracted audiences from around the Mahoning Valley. *Courtesy of the author.*

Below: Cars crowd in for a double feature under the stars at the Sky-Hi. *Courtesy of Vince Guerrieri.*

The Northside Drive-In was the last operating non-adult theater in Youngstown when it closed in 1989. *Courtesy of Mahoning Valley Historical Society.*

to "exploitation" and horror flicks—all the better to appeal to teens and young adults on date night.

Mark Hackett saw many of the horror, sci-fi and exploitation films shown at the Sky-Hi during the 1980s. "Sky-Hi had a monolithic screen tower that was more Art Deco, and it was three dimensional—it wasn't just a white slab on girders….I remember they had a guy who sat back by the tree line in a folding chair. He just sat there and busted cars that were coming in with people hidden in their trunks."

In 1948, Peter Wellman opened his second outdoor theater, the Northside Drive-In, off Belmont Avenue on the outskirts of Youngstown. Smaller than either the Sky-Hi or the Southside, it could hold five hundred cars. At the Northside, Wellman hosted midnight "spook shows" and "dusk to dawn shows," which featured five different films; cartoons and newsreels preceded all movies. The Northside also included "Kidde Land," a playground for young children. (Playgrounds were ubiquitous for years at drive-ins until insurance premiums and litigious parents whittled their numbers.)

Less than two months after the premiere of the Northside, Wellman opened the Westside Drive-In, the third of his three outdoor theaters. Located in the suburb of Austintown, the Westside was the smallest, with a capacity of 450 cars. Unlike its later years, the theater predominately showed mainstream films well into the 1960s, including *The Man Who Shot Liberty Valance*, *The Birds* and *El Cid*. After the end of the Motion Picture Production Code and the dawning of the 1970s, the Westside became known for showing exploitation and even adult films.

The immense difficulties facing drive-ins during the 1980s brought down Mahoning County's outdoor theaters. With suburban developments encroaching and increasing costs plaguing theaters, the dominoes began to fall. The Southside Drive-In closed at the end of the 1984 season; a year later, Victory Christian Center purchased the old Sky-Hi property. With steady residential growth occurring around the Westside Drive-In, management began to face complaints from local residents.

"The area was originally wilderness, but as it became more built up, we became more restricted," former operator William Petrych remarked in 1987. "We haven't had any neighbors complain on a *Rambo*-type thing, but if there was any nudity at all, we couldn't show it, and certain pictures play better at drive-ins."[121]

In 1989, three years after the Westside closed, workers began removing the marquee at the Northside Drive-In, which went dark at the end of that summer. A November 1989 fire destroyed much of the old ozoner, and the entire property was razed in 1990—erasing the last Youngstown-area drive-in from the landscape.

Trumbull County Drive-Ins

Youngstown's hardtop theaters were the most impressive in the Mahoning Valley, but Trumbull County and Warren showcased the longest-lasting drive-in theaters. Dating back to the early 1940s, the area still boasts two outdoor theaters, long after Youngstown's vanished from the scene. Today, the Elm Road Triple Drive-In and the Skyway allow a new generation of moviegoers to experience outdoor movies in the comfort of their automobiles.

Along with the short-lived Outdoor Auto Theater, the generically named Drive In Theatre was one of the first in the Mahoning Valley, opening four miles east of Warren on State Route 422 in 1940. Later renamed the Howland Drive-In, it resembled the Westside Drive-In in size. At that time, only farmland and green space surrounded the bright lights of the new ozoner. Designed with the latest technological developments in mind, the property featured ten curved ramps facing a screen forty feet high and thirty feet wide. Initially, mostly soft drinks were served at the concession area, as well as at individual cars; admission cost thirty-five cents for adults, with children admitted free.

Owner J.S. Cangney spent most of his career in the movie business, having worked for Warner Brothers and Schine Theaters, as well as having run movie houses in Painesville, Bryan and Chagrin Falls, Ohio. Cangney paid particularly close attention to outdoor theaters in Los Angeles, Detroit, Miami and Cleveland, looking to bring the latest in design and technology to the Niles area. Engineers from New York and Cleveland installed the Western Electric projection and the sound amplification system. The *Warren Tribune* ran an unusually large feature on the new drive-in and proudly referred to the "quick public acceptance of the novel theater."[122]

The Howland Drive-In, originally called simply the Drive In Theatre, was the first in Trumbull County. *Courtesy of Ron Flaviano.*

In later years, the Skyway and Elm Road Drive-Ins dominated Warren and Trumbull County. Built one year apart from each other, they have consistently attracted audiences for decades. Both theaters are perfect examples of thriving drive-ins in Ohio, a state that boasts (along with Pennsylvania) the second-highest number in the country.

In the summer of 1950, the Elm Road Drive-In opened in Warren under the helm of Stephen Hreno, a welding foreman turned entrepreneur. It marked the beginning of a family-run enterprise that continues to this day. Hreno originally planned to build a roller skating rink on Elm Road in Warren after purchasing property in 1948; however, a trip to Rainbow Gardens in Pennsylvania changed his mind, according to his son, Robert. "The town had a skating rink and a drive-in theater," he later remembered. "We went to look at the parking lots on a Saturday night and there were a lot more cars at the drive-in than there were at the skating rink. That's how we decided to build the drive-in."[123]

The 1950s were kind to the Hrenos' new enterprise, and the theater prospered. On the tenth anniversary of its opening in 1960, Stephen passed away. Yet the Elm Road continued to thrive along with the nearly 5,800 other drive-ins that existed in the 1960s, the golden age for outdoor theaters. Robert continued to run the business along with his mother, Mary, making additional investments even as drive-ins declined nationally. Eventually, another screen and an enlarged concession area were added in 1979. (Today, there are three screens.) Like the Sky-Hi, Robert also installed electric heaters. This allowed the drive-in to operate year round from 1965 to 1979. Beginning in 1983, moviegoers could hear the theater's audio through their car radios, a major improvement over the old individual car speakers attached to poles.

During the 1960s and 1970s, drive-ins relied on horror, science fiction and other second-run films. The decline of those genres and the arrival of home video seriously affected business. "By the time movies were in second run, many of the same movies were also on video, which cut into profits," Robert Hreno emphasized during a 1995 interview. "As for the B movies like *Godzilla*, *Night of the Living Dead* and [*Texas*] *Chainsaw Massacre*, they just don't make those types of movies anymore."[124]

The increasing costs of acquiring films during the 1980s and early 1990s wiped out drive-ins across the country and seriously affected Elm Road's business. The theater began to rely more on profits generated from concessions, which in 2016 included everything from pizza to hand-dipped ice cream. Yet while its competitors gradually vanished under pressure from development, the Elm Road Triple Drive-In continues to thrive.

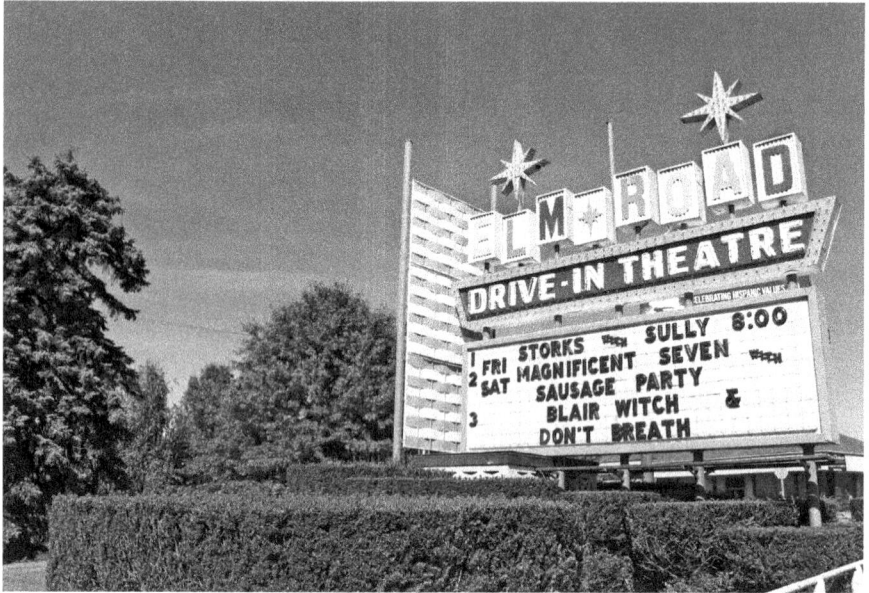

The Elm Road Drive-In and the Skyway continue the Mahoning Valley outdoor movie tradition today. *Photo by the author.*

The Skyway Drive-In, located on Leavitt Road in Warren and currently operated by Brian DeCiancio, has also successfully survived the many challenges facing drive-ins over the years. When it first opened in 1949, Skyway was one of six outdoor theaters in the Mahoning Valley and is the oldest surviving drive-in in the area. The drive-in now has the largest screen in northeastern Ohio and western Pennsylvania and was the first outdoor theater in the region to convert to digital in 2013. Like the Elm Road, it weathered many storms.

In 1987, Dave Albright, owner of the Howland Drive-In, noted that the theater's location across from the Eastwood Mall and the Great East Plaza made it a prime candidate for closure. "The land is not under its best and highest use at the present time," Albright explained. "If I had to predict, I would say within five years the Howland Drive-In won't be there."[125] His prediction turned out to be correct, and many wondered if Skyway would share its fate.

During the 1960s and 1970s, it was not uncommon for eight hundred cars to pack into the Skyway; during the late 1980s, a whole week with a total of eight hundred was considered good business. In order to better compete, management focused on quality first-run films and amenities, such as a playground—one of the few drive-ins that still features such an attraction. A flea market operated on the premises for many years, keeping the property active during the day on weekends. Today, the flea market is gone, but a 2,600-square-foot "Laser Storm" arena is now open on the premises year round. The Skyway and the Elm Road Triple Drive-Ins, successfully navigating the changing times, are sure to keep the long legacy of outdoor movies in the Mahoning Valley alive for years to come.

The Decline of Urban Theaters and the Rise of Plaza and Mall Cinemas

When developer Edward J. DeBartolo began readying his Greater Boardman Plaza for its 1951 grand opening, a premier Youngstown realtor was overheard saying, "I'll give this place six months to fold."[126] Instead, it marked the beginning of a retail shift from Youngstown's downtown to the city's suburbs. In 1958, the Liberty Plaza became part of this shift. Shopping options were now expanding, not just in the city itself, as was the case with the Uptown shopping district, but throughout outlying areas. Suburban residents could now avoid making trips to stores in downtown, which increasingly drained retail traffic and revenues from the central business district.

Although the downtown theaters continued to dominate during the 1950s, plaza theaters rose in the 1960s to challenge their grip on area moviegoers. In 1963, a new cinema opened as part of a six-unit addition to the Boardman Plaza. Another opened the next year in the Liberty Plaza. The Lincoln Knolls Plaza Theater opened on the outskirts of Youngstown in 1963. With 825 seats, it posed another threat to the downtown movie houses. Along with the popularity of drive-ins, plaza cinemas marked the beginning of the end for city theaters.

The cinemas in Liberty, Lincoln Knolls and Boardman were part of the growing Broumas Theaters Inc., headquartered in Silver Springs, Maryland. Former Youngstowner John G. Broumas headed the chain, and despite having properties in six different states, he focused the business in and around his former hometown. His father was a Greek immigrant who made his name operating the first restaurant on Central Square in Youngstown and the city's famed Manhattan Café. John sought to match his success with the theater business. But despite his ambitions, Broumas Theaters declared bankruptcy in 1967. However, the end of the chain had little effect on suburban theaters. They only grew more popular as cinemas opened in new indoor shopping malls.

Edward J. DeBartolo's Southern Park Mall further revolutionized local retail when it opened in 1970. Employing more than 2,000 people, it housed space for 101 stores in well over 1 million square feet of retail space. Much like the plazas, patrons expected to be able to attend a movie during their shopping excursions, so a new single-screen cinema (later divided into two) opened at Southern Park. With seating for 940, the theater was equipped for 70mm Todd-AO projection and Cinemascope. The interior was dressed in warm tones with the latest in modern comfort. Moviegoers found parking readily available, and the theater remained open after mall hours. As a first-run cinema, there were always long lines on the weekend.

Although it was billed as a "luxury theater," the cinema lacked the grandeur and ornamentation of the downtown movie palaces. While not as bare bones as many of today's multiplexes, it remained a modern theater without a distinct individual style. Yet going out to the movies in the 1970s remained a special event, and patrons dressed accordingly. "People would get more dressed up than they do today," former employee Sally Freaney noted. "It wasn't to the extent of what you'd see at theaters in the '50s or '60s, but it was still a little bit special to be there. The female employees wore skirts, the men wore tuxes and the assistant managers always wore suits and ties."

One year before the Southern Park opened, the massive Eastwood Mall debuted in Niles. Described as "Space Age" in size, it completely redefined shopping in Trumbull County. The 1,113,000-square-foot mall hosted familiar names such as McKelvey's, Montgomery Ward, A&P and the "million dollar" Cherry's Top O' the Mall restaurant and nightclub. In addition, a one-thousand-seat Loews Cinema opened. Located directly above F.W. Woolworth, it quickly became the leading theater in the Warren area—*The Poseidon Adventure*, *The Towering Inferno*, *One Flew Over the Cuckoo's Nest* and *Jaws* were among the many hits featured.

"When they first built that theater, it was a very plush place," former employee William Costas explained. "People dressed up to go to the movies. I was an usher, and we wore tuxedos. Dressed up in a tuxedo, you feel like you're somebody important. We used to direct people to their seats."[127]

Rochester, New York interior designer Joseph Schuler used a nontraditional color palette for the cinema's interior. "It was very, very 1970s," Ron Flaviano recalled. "The interior was very blue, and the carpet was blue. It was like walking into a swimming pool. On the upper parts of the wall they had blue,

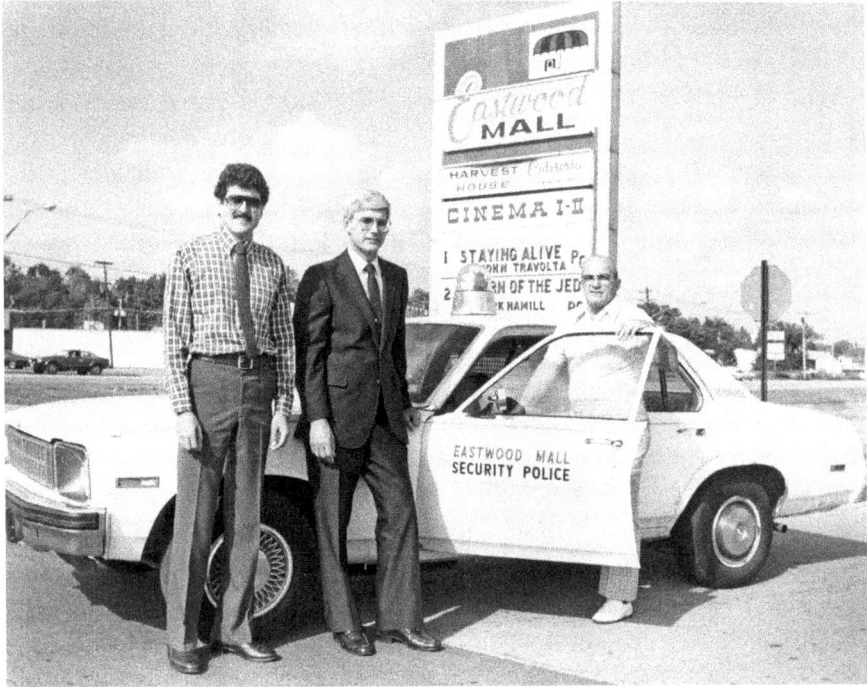

Loews Cinema at Eastwood Mall symbolized the departure from traditional downtown movie houses and neighborhood theaters. *Courtesy of the* Warren Tribune.

monochromatic images of famous movie stars like Marilyn Monroe, Clark Gable and Vivien Leigh."

Just as the plaza theaters drew patrons away from traditional urban theaters, the Eastwood Mall cinema drew moviegoers from plaza theaters and the last of the dying downtown movie houses. "The thing about Eastwood is that it attracted people from Liberty and western Pennsylvania, not to mention Trumbull County in general," local historian Mark Peyko emphasized. "It attracted people who usually went to movies at the Liberty Plaza."

While suburban cinemas thrived, Youngstown's old theaters gradually closed. It was a reflection of not just increased competition from cinemas in the outlying areas but also from television and drive-ins. The general decay of the city—increasingly regarded as dangerous—also had a profound impact on Youngstown theaters. After 1970, only the Paramount remained open downtown. By 1973, it was a grindhouse—pumping out a steady stream of blaxploitation and kung-fu films. The Paramount occasionally showed pornographic movies like *Revenge of the Motorcycle Mamma* before it ultimately closed in late 1975. And the adult film business quickly came to dominate what was left of Youngstown's theaters.

With the end of the Motion Picture Production Code and the dawning of the Age of Aquarius, adult-oriented films increasingly appeared, and local cinemas, struggling to survive, converted to adult theaters: the Mahoning Theater on the west side became the Mahoning Follies; the old Wellman Theater in Girard became Cinema I; and Joe Shagrin's former theater, the Foster, became an adult cinema. The owners of the New Park Burlesk opened the Palace Theater in the 1970s, an adult cinema and dance club on Market Street. Local officials immediately sought to crack down on these establishments.

In 1974, Youngstown adopted ordinances restricting adult bookstores and movie theaters to locations more than five hundred feet away from private residences, schools, libraries, parks and playgrounds. In addition, police repeatedly raided local establishments after the State of Ohio passed several obscenity statutes in the early 1970s. These included the Foster, Mahoning Follies and the New Park Burlesk—where adult films were shown and sold on 8mm reels. The city permanently shut down the Palace on Market Street. In 1974, officials raided the Westside Drive-In, closing it temporarily and arresting the manager. Several local religious organizations also targeted adult theaters over the years, especially the Foster.

The Mafia apparently infiltrated the pornography business as well, according to the *New York Times*. In October 1974, police found an abandoned, bloodstained car not far from Youngstown in the organized crime stronghold of Campbell. It belonged to Philip "Fleegle" Mainer, a handler for the mob's adult film distribution network; his body was never found.[128]

Fourteen theaters and one burlesque house served Youngstown in 1946. By 1986, only the Uptown remained. Late that year, the city, fearing that the theater might become a pornographic movie house, facilitated a loan for businessman James Wilcox to purchase it. He operated the venue until 1989, when Easy Street Productions converted the Uptown to a live theater. The city of Youngstown's long tradition of motion pictures, which began in the dark nickelodeons of the early twentieth century, ended in the late summer of 1989 after the closing of the Northside Drive-In.

No legitimate movie theaters, aside from drive-ins, exist in either Warren or Youngstown today. Regal Cinemas and Cinemark Theaters—large, generic, multi-screen complexes—eventually replaced the suburban plaza and mall cinemas. The primitive nickelodeons, the palatial downtown picture palaces and the neighborhood theaters have all receded into the past. The burlesque houses with their baggy-pants comedians and dancing girls are a product of another era. The classical opera houses and their vaudevillians no longer grace the downtowns.

Today, theaters compete with a vast array of entertainment options: Netflix, YouTube, portable electronic devices of every variety and home movies on demand. Yet the classic Powers Auditorium continues to provide a venue for live performances, and the Youngstown Playhouse, one of the oldest community theaters in the country, still produces the very best local stage productions. The summer lights of the Elm Road Triple and Skyway Drive-Ins beckon patrons looking to enjoy double features under a canopy of stars. They all invite us to enjoy the ongoing theatrical tradition of the Mahoning Valley.

NOTES

Introduction

1. Cecil B. Brown, "Audiences Sit on Their Hands," *Youngstown Vindicator*, August 31, 1930.
2. Butsch, *Making of American Audiences*, 119.
3. Mark C. Peyko, "Notes from Youngstown: The Angry Voice of a City Left Behind," *New York Times*, February 28, 2002.
4. Robinson, *From Peep Show to Palace*, 90.
5. *Youngstown Vindicator*, "Youngstown Is Some City," July 30, 1910.
6. Ibid., "Youngstown Has Second-Best Gain of Ohio Cities," June 17, 1930.
7. Charles A. Leedy, "Youngstown Show Center When There Were Shows; Now Movies Hold Sway," *Youngstown Telegraph*, June 29, 1931.

Part 1

8. *Youngstown Vindicator*, "The Excelsior Building Association," May 2, 1910.
9. William L. Rook, "Greatest American Thespians Have Trod City's Stages," *Youngstown Vindicator*, March 27, 1938.
10. Robinson, *From Peep Show to Palace*, 33.
11. *Youngstown Vindicator*, "Cheap Theaters and Picture Shows Earning Fortunes for Promoters," February 2, 1907.
12. *Moving Picture World*, October 7, 1907, 593.
13. Butsch, *Making of American Audiences*, 141.

14. *Moving Picture World*, April 1907, 88.

15. Rhodes, *Perils of Moviegoing in America*, 87.

16. Robinson, *From Peep Show to Palace*, 98.

17. *Youngstown Vindicator*, "Moving Pictures the Theater's New Competitor," April 11, 1909.

18. *Moving Picture World*, "That Youngstown License," April 1910.

19. *Motography*, "Youngstown Ministers Report," April 1911, 16.

20. *Moving Picture World*, "Public Opinion Against Exhibition of Morbid Subjects," April 1908, 312.

21. Abel, *Americanizing the Movies*, 52–53.

22. Robinson, *From Peep Show to Palace*, 90.

23. Leone, *Rose Street*, 208.

24. Sperling and Millner, *Hollywood Be Thy Name*, 57.

25. *Pittsburgh Press*, "Movie Magnate Once Held Job as Suit Salesman Here," July 2, 1929.

26. Warner, *My First Hundred Years in Hollywood*, 55.

27. *Pittsburgh Press*, "Movie Magnate Once Held Job."

28. *Youngstown Vindicator*, "Once a Vindicator Newsie, Now World Famed Producer," December 9, 1923.

29. *Variety*, "Jack L. Warner's Death Closes Out Pioneer Clan of 'Talkies,'" September 13, 1978, 2.

30. Warner, *My First Hundred Years in Hollywood*, 42.

31. *Moving Picture World*, "Youngstown, O.," October 12, 1911, 650.

32. Sperling and Milner, *Hollywood Be Thy Name*, 111.

33. Esther Hamilton, "Amazing Career of the Warner Bros.," *Youngstown Vindicator*, August 19, 1938.

34. Hynes, interview by Carol Shaffer Mills.

35. *Niles Times*, May 1, 1923.

Part 2

36. *Youngstown Telegram*, "First Burlesque Show Shocked Town," February 11, 1931.

37. Zemeckis, *Behind the Burly Q*, 4.

38. *Youngstown Vindicator*, "Strippers Can't Show All Here, Kane States, in 'Tassel Battle,'" August 26, 1950.

39. Ibid., "Park Theater Opens Its Doors to the Public," February 5, 1901.

40. Shteir, *Striptease*, 205–6.

41. Ibid.
42. Paquette, *Small Town Girl*, 83.
43. Fred Childress, "At the Theaters," *Youngstown Vindicator*, November 20, 1949.
44. Seymour Rothman, "Ex-Ecdysiast Rose La Rose Follows Burlesque in Death," *Toledo Blade*, July 28, 1972.
45. *Youngstown Vindicator*, "City Won't Ease Burlesque Bans," February 24, 1953.
46. Ibid., "Council Shuns Move to Ban Girlie Shows," June 19, 1958.
47. Ibid., editorial, February 20, 1959.
48. Ibid., "May Padlock Burlesque," May 12, 1960.
49. Joe Tronzo, "Burlesque Shows Innocent Compared to Today," *Allegheny Times*, October 30, 1988.
50. *Youngstown Vindicator*, "New Burlesque Theater Set for Old Hotel Site," September 20, 1968.
51. Fred Childress, "All New Park Theater Has Burlesque Friday," *Youngstown Vindicator*, March 2, 1969.
52. *Gettysburg Times*, "Stripper Faces 3 Months in Jail," October 30, 1963.
53. Mike Kalina, "Old Burlesque Fading with Stars," *Pittsburgh Post-Gazette*, December 25, 1978.

Part 3

54. Testa, interview by William Kish.
55. *Youngstown Vindicator*, "State Militia in the Streets," January 8, 1916.
56. Kish, interview by William Kish.
57. Ernest Brown Jr., "Chic It Wasn't, but Monkey's Nest Was Home, and More, to Its People," *Youngstown Vindicator*, August 14, 1977.
58. Testa, interview by William Kish.
59. Pavlansky, *Images of America: Campbell*.
60. Tarcy, interview by William Kish.
61. Tommy Black, "He Made Movie Theaters His Lifelong Work, Love," *Birmingham News*, October 28, 1980.
62. Bruno, *Steelworker Alley*, 26.
63. *Struthers Journal*, "New Ritz Theater Will Open for First Show Tuesday Night," April 30, 1937.
64. Linda and Al Tombo, interview by Scott Smith.
65. Peyko, *Remembering Youngstown*, 48.

66. *Youngstown Vindicator*, "Dignitaries Help Canfield Place Stone of New Center," May 14, 1936.
67. *Motography*, April–December 1911.
68. E. Ross Mateer, "Girard as I Remember It," available at Girard Free Library, 10.
69. *Niles Daily Times*, "New Building to House Theater, 4 Storerooms; Girard Building Grows," September 18, 1936.
70. Mike Varveris, "Peter M. Wellman, Legend in Our Time?," *Niles Daily Times*, March 13, 1969.
71. *Niles Daily Times*, "Wellman Sells Girard Theaters," May 15, 1959.
72. Varveris, "Peter M. Wellman."
73. *Girard News*, "Residents Give Varied Opinions on Showing of Adult Movies in Girard," August 7, 1969.
74. *Niles Times*, "Theater May Close, No Local Support," July 3, 1970.
75. Also see Posey, *Lost Youngstown*, 66.
76. Donald Hegfield, interview by Dorothy Bullock.
77. Ibid.
78. Fuller-Seeley, "Dish Night at the Movies," 264.
79. Lark, *Blast from the Past*, 65.

Part 4

80. Wendell F. Lauth, "Flickering Films Attracted Hordes to Nickelodeons," *Warren Tribune*, October 8, 1984.
81. Ibid.
82. *Moving Picture World*, January–March 1915.
83. *Warren Tribune*, "Show Stage May Be Added to Theater," January 9, 1923.
84. Ibid., "Mayor to Formally Open New $250,000 Daniel Theater Here," May 19, 1942.
85. Ibid.
86. Ibid., editorial, April 19, 1958.
87. Chris Columbus, "Warren Homecoming 2016," Facebook, https://www.facebook.com/warrenhomecoming/videos/521222624746058/?hc_ref=PAGES_TIMELINE.

Part 5

88. Polly Hossel, "Old-Timers Watch Sad-Eyed as Stage at 'Hip' Is Razed," *Youngstown Vindicator*, November 24, 1935.
89. M.R. Shohet, editorial, *Youngstown Vindicator*, July 20, 1924.
90. Watkins, *Dancing with Strangers*, 132–33, 147, 151.
91. Ibid., 112.
92. *Youngstown Vindicator*, "Need Sweeping Change for E. Federal Property," editorial, February 1, 1959.
93. Ibid., "Cameo Theater Opening Today," January 22, 1928.
94. Ibid., "Todd-AO Comes to Youngstown," May 29, 1957.
95. Steel Strings, "List of 1975 Tomorrow Club Shows," entry posted on September 13, 2012, https://yosteelstrings.wordpress.com/2012/09/13/list-of-1975-tomorrow-club-shows.
96. Case, *Elvis Presley's Hips*, 39.
97. Hudson, *Diary of a Punk*, 21.
98. Manning, interview by D. Scott Van Horn.
99. *Youngstown Vindicator*, "Keith-Albee House Opened," March 16, 1926.
100. Ibid., "Promise New Era of Vodvil," September 7, 1929.
101. Elser, interview by Terence M. Lynch.
102. William FitzGerald, "Glenn Miller's Orchestra Draws Big Crowd at Palace," *Youngstown Vindicator*, August 5, 1942.
103. Simon, *Big Bands*, 4.
104. Peyko, *Remembering Youngstown*, 85.
105. Youngstown City Planning Commission, *Toward a Downtown Plan*.
106. Ibid., *Economic Analysis of the Central Business District*.
107. Carl Straley, letter to the editor, *Youngstown Vindicator*, December 30, 1971.
108. Catesby B. Cannon Jr., "Will Raze Palace and Sear Bldg.," *Youngstown Vindicator*, April 10, 1964.
109. *Town Talk*, May 1931.
110. *Youngstown Vindicator*, "Youngstown Steps Out at Opening of Warner," May 15, 1931.
111. Robert G. Batman, "Dedicate New Warner House to Serve City," *Youngstown Telegraph*, May 15, 1931.
112. Joseph L. Heffernan, "The Hungry City: A Mayor's Experience with Unemployment," *Atlantic Monthly*, May 1932.
113. *Youngstown Vindicator*, "Warner Brothers Plan to Build $100,000 North Side Theater," December 17, 1940.

114. Fred Childress, "Built as Memorial to Family," *Youngstown Vindicator*, February 18, 1968.

115. Vargo, interview by the author.

116. *Youngstown Vindicator*, "Curtain Drops Last Time for Warner," February 28, 1968.

117. Ibid., editorial, September 15, 1968.

Part 6

118. Segrave, *Drive-In Theaters*, vii.

119. Ibid., 85.

120. DiCicco, *Running with God*, 108.

121. John Lis, "Final Screens?," *Warren Tribune*, July 19, 1987.

122. *Warren Tribune*, "Unique Drive-In Theater Opens Tomorrow," August 9, 1940.

123. Cynthia Vinarsky, "The Last Picture Show," *Youngstown Vindicator*, August 17, 1992.

124. *Youngstown Vindicator*, "A Successful Plot: Stick with Family," June 18, 1995.

125. Andy Gray, "Lighting Up the Sky," *Warren Tribune*, May 22, 1987.

126. Gary W. Diedrichs, "Edward J. DeBartolo: The Pharaoh from Youngstown," *Cleveland Magazine*, July 1976.

127. Nancilynn Gatta, "When Movies Were an Event," *Warren Tribune*, December 27, 2013.

128. Nicholas Gage, "Organized Crime Reaps Huge Profits from Dealing in Pornographic Films," *New York Times*, October 12, 1975.

BIBLIOGRAPHY

Books

Abel, Richard. *Americanizing the Movies and "Movie-Mad" Audiences, 1910–1914.* Berkeley: University of California Press, 2006.

Bruno, Robert. *Steelworker Alley: How Class Works in Youngstown.* Ithaca, NY: Cornell University Press, 1999.

Butsch, Richard. *The Making of American Audiences: From Stage to Television, 1750–1990.* Cambridge, UK: Cambridge University Press, 2000.

Case, Susana H. *Elvis Presley's Hips and Mick Jagger's Lips.* Shantou, CH: Anaphora, 2012.

DiCicco, Patrick R. *Running with God, an Autobiography by Patrick DiCicco: A Spiritual Journey through the Streets of Youngstown and the Sea of Life.* New York: iUniverse Inc., n.d.

Fuller-Seeley, Kathryn H. "Dish Night at the Movies." In *Looking Past the Screen: Case Studies in American Film History and Method.* Edited by Jon Lewis and Eric Smoodin. Durham, NC: Duke University Press, 2007.

Hudson, Mike. *Diary of a Punk: Life and Death in the Pagans.* Niagara Falls, NY: Tuscarora Books, 2008.

Lark, Mary Ann. *Blast from the Past: '40s, '50s and More.* Raleigh, NC: Lulu, 2009.

Leone, Carmen J. *Rose Street: A Family Story.* Youngstown, OH, 1996.

Paquette, Jack K. *Small Town Girl: And Other Stories About Ordinary People Who Led Extraordinary Lives.* Bloomington, IN: Xlibris, 2013.

Pavlansky, Joseph. *Images of America: Campbell*. Charleston, SC: Arcadia Publishing, 2016.

Peyko, Mark C., ed. *Remembering Youngstown: Tales from the Mahoning Valley*. Charleston, SC: The History Press, 2009.

Posey, Sean T. *Lost Youngstown*. Charleston, SC: The History Press, 2016.

Rhodes, Gary D. *The Perils of Moviegoing in America, 1896–1950*. New York: Continuum International Publishing Group, 2012.

Robinson, David. *From Peep Show to Palace: The Birth of American Film*. New York: Columbia University Press, 1996.

Segrave, Kerry. *Drive-In Theaters: A History from Their Inception in 1933*. Jefferson, NC: McFarland & Company, 1992.

Shteir, Rachel. *Striptease: The Untold History of the Girlie Show*. Oxford, UK: Oxford University Press, 2004.

Simon, George T. *The Big Bands*. New York: Schirmer Trade Books, 2012.

Sperling, Cass Warner, and Cork Millner. *Hollywood Be Thy Name: The Warner Brothers Story*. Lexington: University of Kentucky Press, 1998.

Warner, Jack L. *My First Hundred Years in Hollywood*. Hollywood, CA: Random House, 1965.

Watkins, Mel. *Dancing with Strangers: A Memoir*. New York: Simon and Schuster, 1998.

Zemeckis, Leslie. *Behind the Burly Q: The Story of Burlesque in America*. New York: Skyhorse Publishing, 2014.

City Reports

Youngstown City Planning Commission. *Economic Analysis of the Central Business District*. 1963.

———. *Toward a Downtown Plan: Preliminary Planning Proposals*. March 1960.

Interviews

Brayer, Denny. Interview by the author, June 2016.

Carlton, Jack. Interview by the author, June 2016.

Cavanaugh, Doris, and Frank Cavanaugh. Interview by the author, March 2016.

DeCicco, Bill. Interview by the author, August 2015.

Delio, Frank. Interview by the author, December 2014.

Flaviano, Mary Ann. Interview by the author, July 2016.
Flaviano, Ron. Interview by the author, December 2015.
Freaney, Sally. Interview by the author, September 2016.
Garfield, Sharon Williams. Interview by the author, November 2015.
Hackett, Mark. Interview by the author, June 2016.
Hall, George. Interview by the author, January 2016.
Hughes, Jaime. Interview by the author, February 2016.
Jones, Bryan, and Roger Jones. Interview by the author, February 2016.
Lark, Mary Ann. Interview by the author, January 2016.
Mageros, Emanuel. Interview by the author, February 2016.
Mauzy, Candace. Interview by the author, April 2016.
Moore, Liz. Interview by the author, February 2015.
Petrello, Mike. Interview by the author, January 2016.
Peyko, Mark. Interview by the author, December 2015.
Peyko, William S. Interview by the author, May 2016.
Posey, Fred. Interview by the author, August 2016.
Roncone, Mike. Interview by the author, March 2016.
Rowe, Thomas. Interview by the author, September 2016.
Scarsella, Richard. Interview by the author, June 2015.
Vargo, Bob. Interview by the author, July 2015.
Wengler, Helga. Interview by the author, September 2016.

Newspapers

Allegheny Times. 1988.
Atlantic Monthly. 1932.
Birmingham News. 1980.
Cleveland Magazine. 1976.
Gettysburg Times. 1963.
Girard News. 1969.
New York Times. 1975–2002.
Niles Daily Times. 1936, 1959, 1969.
Niles Times. 1923–70.
Pittsburgh Post-Gazette. 1978.
Pittsburgh Press. 1929.
Struthers Journal. 1937.
Toledo Blade. 1972.
Variety. 1978.

Warren Tribune. 1923–2013.
Youngstown Telegram. 1931.
Youngstown Vindicator. 1901–95.

Oral Histories

Elser, Donald. Interview by Terence M. Lynch, May 12, 1977. Transcript. History of Youngstown State University. OH 120. Youngstown State University Oral History Program, Youngstown, OH.

Hegfield, Donald. Interview by Dorothy Bullock, November 12, 1975. Transcript. Hubbard Bicentennial History. OH 822. Youngstown State University Oral History Program, Youngstown, OH.

Hynes, Jack. Interview by Carol Shaffer Mills, January 26, February 3 and June 11, 1982. Transcript. Theater People from Ohio. OH 1579. Youngstown State University Oral History Program, Youngstown, OH.

Kish, Billy. Interview by William M. Kish, July 15, 1989. Transcript. Campbell, Ohio, During the 1930s and 1940s. OH 1237. Youngstown State University Oral History Program, Youngstown, OH.

Manning, Edward C. Interview by D. Scott Van Horn, May 14, 1986. Transcript. Youngstown in the 1920s and 1930s. OH 666. Youngstown State University Oral History Program, Youngstown, OH.

Tarcy, Helen E. Interview by William M. Kish, July 11, 1989. Transcript. Campbell, Ohio, During the 1930s and 1940s. OH 1238. Youngstown State University Oral History Program, Youngstown, OH.

Testa, Charles. Interview by William Kish, July 14, 1989. Transcript. Campbell, Ohio, During the 1930s and 1940s. OH 1239. Youngstown State University Oral History Program, Youngstown, OH.

Tombo, Al, and Linda Tombo. Interview by Scott Smith, November 26, 1991. Transcript. Idora Park Project. OH 1472. Youngstown State University Oral History Program, Youngstown, OH.

Trade Journals

Motography. 1911.
Moving Picture World. 1907–15.

INDEX

ABOUT THE AUTHOR

Photo by the author.

S ean T. Posey is a freelance writer, photographer and historian. He holds a bachelor's degree in photojournalism from the Academy of Art University in San Francisco and a master's degree in history from Youngstown State University. His work has been featured in a variety of publications, including *Citylab*, *Salon* and *Bill Moyers and Company*, as well as in the books *Car Bombs to Cookie Tables: The Youngstown Anthology* and the *Pittsburgh Anthology*, both by Belt Publishing. The History Press released Sean's first book, *Lost Youngstown*, in 2016.

www.ingramcontent.com/pod-product-compliance
Lightning Source LLC
Chambersburg PA
CBHW070836100426
42813CB00003B/643